Mastering

CorelDraw 2025

The Definitive Guide to Creating Breathtaking
Designs, Graphics, and Illustrations Like a Pro

Jaxon Strathmore

Disclaimer and Terms of Use

The author and publisher of this book and the accompanying materials have used their best efforts in preparing this book. The author and publisher make no representation or warranties with respect to the accuracy, applicability, fitness, or completeness of the contents of this book. The information contained in this book is strictly for informational purposes. Therefore, if you wish to apply the ideas contained in this book, you are taking full responsibility for your actions.

Printed in the United States of America

TABLE OF CONTENTS

INTRODUCTION TO CORELDRAW

CorelDRAW, a dynamic and influential vector graphics editor, has made an indelible impact on the field of graphic design. It was developed by Corel Corporation. This software, which was launched in 1989, has developed into a comprehensive array of creative tools, garnering it the reputation of a go-to platform for designers worldwide. CorelDRAW is built to deliver precise and flexible design capabilities using vector graphics. Unlike raster images, which rely on pixels, vector graphics use mathematical formulas to define shapes. This ensures designs stay sharp and clear no matter how much you resize them. This makes CorelDRAW ideal for tasks like creating logos, illustrations, and intricate layouts. Its user-friendly interface is a key advantage, making it accessible to both beginners and seasoned designers. The software also boosts productivity with tools like LiveSketch and the Smart Drawing feature. These tools, powered by AI, streamline the design process and make it more efficient. Furthermore, CorelDRAW is distinguished by its adaptability, which enables it to seamlessly accommodate a wide range of design requirements. Designers discover a platform that is both adaptable and robust in CorelDRAW, regardless of whether they are producing print materials, web graphics, or social media assets. CorelDRAW remains an essential tool for transforming creative visions into captivating visual realities, thanks to its dedication to staying at the vanguard of design technology and its regular updates.

Features of CorelDRAW

CorelDRAW provides a wide range of software options to meet the diverse requirements of designers. CorelDRAW Graphics Suite is a comprehensive suite designed for professional designers, while CorelDRAW Standard is aimed at enthusiasts. CorelDRAW Essentials offers a simplified version that is particularly well-suited for novice users. The accessibility and scalability of these options are guaranteed for users of all talent levels:

Corel Font Manager

Corel Font Manager is an important part of the CorelDRAW suite, designed to help users manage and organize fonts for smoother design workflows. It allows users to easily explore their font libraries and preview typefaces using customizable sample text. With features like font filtering, searching, and marking, Corel Font Manager makes finding and selecting the right font much simpler. It also supports teamwork by letting users share font collections with others. This tool reflects CorelDRAW's focus on user-friendly design, helping designers efficiently handle fonts and improve the typography in their projects.

AfterShot HDR

AfterShot HDR is a feature of Corel's AfterShot Pro that is specifically designed for High Dynamic Range (HDR) photography. This tool enables photographers to capture and exhibit a wider variety of tones and details in their images. AfterShot HDR enables users to integrate multiple exposures of a scene, combining highlights and shadows to create a visually striking effect. The software guarantees a balanced and convincing HDR result by offering precise control over tonal adjustments. This feature is a critical element of advanced photo editing in AfterShot Pro, as it enables photographers to achieve compelling images with vivid contrasts and vibrant details by enhancing the dynamic range of their photographs.

Corel Photo-Paint

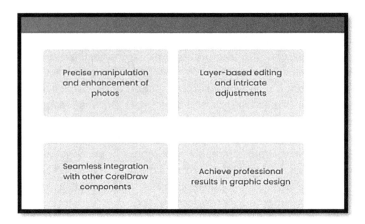

Corel PHOTO-PAINT, part of the CorelDRAW Graphics Suite, is a powerful tool for editing raster images. It is known for its advanced features that let users enhance and modify photos with great accuracy. The software includes a wide range of tools, such as layer-based editing, filters, and brushes, allowing users to make creative changes and detailed adjustments. It works seamlessly with other CorelDRAW tools and supports many file formats, making it a versatile choice for digital artists and photographers. Whether you're retouching photos, designing complex compositions, or adding special effects, Corel PHOTO-PAINT is a go-to tool for achieving professional-quality results in raster-based design.

CorelDraw.app

CorelDRAW.app is the online version of the popular CorelDRAW vector graphics editor. It allows users to create, edit, and collaborate on designs directly through a web browser, removing the need for software installation. The app retains CorelDRAW's powerful features, ensuring smooth integration between the desktop and web versions. With its easy-to-use interface, CorelDRAW.app makes it possible for designers to work on projects and collaborate from anywhere. This tool supports real-time teamwork and offers flexibility, making it ideal for the demands of a mobile and connected design environment. It enhances both the efficiency and collaboration of the design process.

Why Choose CorelDRAW?

CorelDRAW is distinguished by its ability to combine functionality with simplicity. In contrast to certain competitors, it provides a more user-friendly learning curve, rendering it appropriate for novices. Simultaneously, it is furnished with sophisticated capabilities that satisfy the requirements of professional designers. It is the preferred option for digital and print designs due to its emphasis on vector graphics and high-quality output.

Importance of CorelDRAW

CorelDRAW is essential for graphic design, providing a dynamic suite of tools that are suitable for both professionals and novices. Its intuitive interface and robust features, such as vector graphics, facilitate the creation of designs that are both precise and scalable. The visual industry worldwide is influenced by CorelDRAW's indispensable qualities, including its adaptability to a wide range of projects, regular updates, and accessibility. **Various aspects that contribute to the significance of CorelDraw are detailed below:**

1. **Transform Bitmap Images into Vector Graphics**

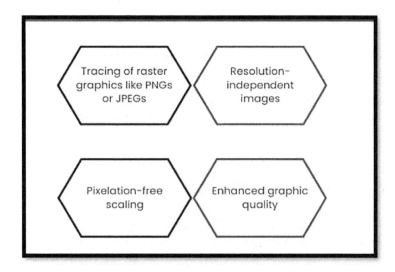

CorelDRAW is a transformative tool for converting bitmap images into vector images. This procedure converts raster graphics, such as JPEGs or PNGs, into scalable vector graphics (SVG). The outcome is a resolution-independent image that allows for precise enlargements without pixelation. CorelDRAW's vectorization tools enable designers to effortlessly enhance the quality and adaptability of their graphics.

2. **Craft Engaging Visuals for Social Media**

CorelDRAW is a game-changing tool for creating visually appealing social media content. CorelDRAW's intuitive tools facilitate the creation of visually appealing posts, including shareable content and attention-grabbing graphics. The software's adaptability guarantees the seamless creation of content for a variety of platforms, enabling businesses and individuals to engage their audience with visually appealing and shareable social media content.

3. **Enhance Image Perspective and Quality**

CorelDRAW is particularly adept at improving the quality and perspective of images. Users can optimize their visual impact by adjusting perspective, refining details, and correcting distortions with sophisticated tools. CorelDRAW's precision allows users to enhance the quality of their images, resulting in visually striking pieces that are both professional and clear, regardless of whether they are used for graphic design or photography.

4. **Produce Documents with a Professional Aesthetic**

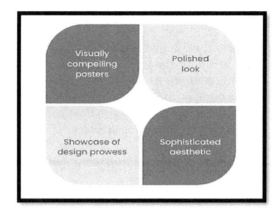

CorelDRAW is essential for the creation of documents that exhibit a professional appearance. Its design and layout tools enable users to generate visually appealing brochures, posters, and other materials. The refined and sophisticated appearance of each document is guaranteed by CorelDRAW, which ensures that it is a testament to the professional design capabilities of its users, from typography to graphic elements.

Applications of CorelDRAW

- **Branding and Identity**: Create logos, business cards, and corporate branding materials.
- **Advertising**: Design banners, posters, and digital ads.
- **Publishing**: Develop layouts for magazines, eBooks, and brochures.
- **Web Graphics**: Design scalable web assets like icons and headers.
- **Clothing and Merchandise**: Produce designs for apparel, promotional items, and packaging.

Who Should Use CorelDRAW?

CorelDRAW is adaptable and can accommodate a diverse audience, such as:
1. **Graphic Designers:** Graphic designers are responsible for the development of intricate vector illustrations and compositions.
2. **Businesses:** The purpose is to develop corporate identities and marketing materials.
3. **Students:** Individuals who are pursuing a degree in digital art or graphic design.
4. **Hobbyists:** Casual users who are interested in experimenting with creative endeavors.

Getting Started with CorelDRAW 2025

For novice users, CorelDRAW offers an intuitive workspace, sample projects, and built-in tutorials to facilitate the first steps. Regardless of whether you are creating a comprehensive illustration, editing a photo, or designing a logo, the software's tools and resources are user-friendly and pleasurable. I am available to provide you with a step-by-step tutorial if you are interested in learning more about a particular feature or workflow in CorelDRAW 2025.

CHAPTER ONE
CORELDRAW OVERVIEW

What's New in CorelDRAW 2025

- **Painterly Brush Tool:** This tool enables the creation of realistic, painterly effects within vector illustrations by combining pixel-based brush strokes that are controlled by vector curves. It provides a diverse selection of brush categories and settings, allowing artists to incorporate intricate details into their designs.
- **Remote Fonts Integration:** CorelDRAW and Corel PHOTO-PAINT now allow users to directly access remote font libraries, such as Google Fonts. This integration streamlines the process of locating and utilizing new fonts without the need to exit the application.
- **Streamlined Non-Destructive Effects Workflow:** The non-destructive bitmap effects workflow has been improved to ensure a more consistent and efficient experience. Users can apply a variety of effects to objects, modify them in real-time, and reorder or toggle them on and off as necessary.
- **Focus Mode:** This function enables designers to concentrate on specific objects or groups within a complex project, thereby enhancing workflow efficiency and reducing distractions. It allows users to make detailed edits to elements without influencing other aspects of the design.
- **Enhanced Print Merge Functionality:** The print merge feature now supports variable data publishing with Excel files and other formats, simplifying the process of creating personalized documents such as business cards and invitations. Variable text, images, and QR codes can be seamlessly integrated into the designs of users.
- **Expanded Template Library:** CorelDRAW Graphics Suite 2025 provides a diverse selection of starting points for a variety of projects, including web graphics and brochures, with access to more than 300 new cloud-based design templates. Designers can customize these templates to meet their unique requirements.
- **User-Requested Enhancements:** In response to user feedback, numerous enhancements have been implemented, such as improved scaling tools for object resizing, improvements to the export procedure for accelerated output, and support for supplementary file formats such as WebP. The objective of these modifications is to enhance overall productivity and simplify the design process.

System Requirements

Minimum System Requirements

1. **Operating System**
   - Windows 11 or Windows 10, 64-bit, with the most recent service packs and updates.
   - The Mac version is available in macOS Ventura (13), macOS Monterey (12), or macOS Big Sur (11).
2. **Processor**
   - A multi-core processor, such as an Intel Core i3 or AMD Ryzen 3, is recommended for optimal performance.
   - Processor with a minimum speed of 2 GHz or higher.
3. **RAM**

- Four gigabytes of RAM is recommended for optimal multitasking and the management of large files, with eight gigabytes or more being preferred.

4. **Graphics Card**
   - A graphics card that is compatible with DirectX 12 and has a minimum of 1 GB of VRAM, with a recommended minimum of 2 GB.
   - Advanced photo editing capabilities necessitate OpenCL 1.2 support.

5. **Storage**
   - A minimum of 5 GB of available hard disk space is required for installation, with additional space required for transient files and content.
   - A Solid-State Drive (SSD) is advised for enhanced performance.

6. **Display**
   - A screen resolution of 1280 x 720 at 100% (96 dpi).
   - The optimal user experience is achieved with a resolution of 1920 x 1080 or higher.

7. **Input Devices**
   - A standard keyboard and mouse or a graphics tablet that is compatible.
   - Stylus that is optional for input that is sensitive to pressure.

8. **Internet**
   - Installation, activation, and access to online features and updates necessitate an internet connection.

9. **Additional Requirements**
   - Microsoft.NET Framework 4.7.2 or a later version for Windows.
   - Devices that support macOS Metal for GPU acceleration.

Recommended System Requirements

For optimal performance, particularly when working on complex designs, large files, or multitasking:

1. **Operating System**
   - The most recent 64-bit versions of Windows or macOS, with all necessary updates installed.

2. **Processor**
   - A multi-core processor such as an Intel Core i7 or AMD Ryzen 7 (or a higher version).

3. **RAM**
   - For high-performance operations, a minimum of 16 GB of RAM is required.

4. **Graphics Card**
   - A dedicated GPU with 4 GB VRAM (e.g., NVIDIA GeForce GTX 1660 or AMD Radeon RX 5600 XT) is required for real-time effects and sophisticated rendering.

5. **Storage**
   - A 1 TB solid-state drive (SSD) is included to facilitate the seamless management of high-resolution projects and ensure rapid storage.

6. **Display**
   - A 4K Ultra-HD monitor for the precise completion of design and editing duties.
   - A multi-monitor configuration to optimize productivity.

Compatibility and Recommendations

- **Hardware:** CorelDRAW is designed to operate efficiently on both desktop and laptop systems; however, professional users are advised to utilize high-end specifications.

- **Peripherals:** Illustrators and designers can benefit from the use of Wacom tablets or other sophisticated drawing devices.
- **Cloud Features:** Users who intend to utilize the CorelDRAW.app or collaboration features should ensure that they have a reliable and rapid internet connection.

Installing CorelDRAW 2025

1. **Preparing for Installation**
   - **Check System Requirements**

Before commencing, confirm that your system satisfies the minimum and recommended specifications for CorelDRAW 2025. This guarantees that the software will function seamlessly following installation.

   - **Secure Your Internet Connection**

To download the installation files, activate the software, and access online features, a reliable internet connection is required.

   - **Uninstall Older Versions (Optional)**

Although CorelDRAW permits the coexistence of multiple versions, the removal of older versions can alleviate potential conflicts and free up disk space.

2. **Downloading CorelDRAW 2025**
   - **Visit the Official Website**

Navigate to the **Downloads** or **Products** section of the official Corel website at **www.coreldraw.com.**

   - **Select the Version**

Select **CorelDRAW Graphics Suite 2025**. You have the option to purchase the complete version or select a trial version, depending on your preference.

   - **Create or Log In to Your Corel Account**
     - Sign up for a complimentary account if you are a new user of Corel.
     - Existing users can access their purchase or trial by logging in.
   - **Download the Installer**

To save the installer file to your computer, click on the download link. The file size will typically fall within the range of 1.5 GB to 2 GB.

3. **Installing CorelDRAW 2025**
   - **Run the Installer**
     - Double-click the **.exe file** that you downloaded on Windows.
     - To access the installer on macOS, double-click the **.dmg file**.
   - **Choose Installation Type**
     - **Typical Installation:** CorelDRAW is installed with the default settings and features.
     - **Custom Installation:** Enables the selection of specific components, such as language bundles or supplementary tools.
   - **Examine the License Agreement**
     - To proceed, please review and approve the End User License Agreement (EULA).
   - **Specify Installation Location**
     - Choose the directory in which CorelDRAW will be installed. The default location is generally adequate for the majority of consumers.
   - **Install Optional Features**
     - You may be required to install supplementary software, including Corel Font Manager and Corel PHOTO-PAINT.

- o Choose the features that are essential to you, but be aware that they can necessitate additional disk space.
  - **Begin Installation**
    - o To initiate the installation procedure, select either the **Install** or **Next** icon. This may require a few minutes, contingent upon the pace of your system.
4. **Activating CorelDraw 2025**
   - **Start the Software**
     - o Open CorelDRAW 2025 from your desktop or applications folder after the installation is finished.
   - **Sign**
     - o Activate the software by logging in with your Corel account credentials.
   - **Enter Your License key**
     - o Enter the license key that was supplied to you during the purchase process if you purchased CorelDRAW.
     - o Trial users should select "Start Trial" to commence using the software for a restricted duration.
   - **Verify Activation**
     - o The software will validate the license key online after it has been entered. CorelDRAW 2025 will be entirely activated upon verification.
5. **Post-Installation Setup**
   - **Download Updates**
     - o Ensure that you have the most recent version of CorelDRAW 2025, which includes issue fixes and new features, by checking for updates.
   - **Set Preferences**
     - o Customize the interface theme, toolbars, and default document templates to align with your workflow.
   - **Tutorials are Accessible**
     - o Investigate the features of CorelDRAW by utilizing the built-in tutorials, assistance files, and online resources.

Troubleshooting Common Issues

- **Slow Installation:** Prioritize the closure of extraneous applications and ensure that there is sufficient disk space available for the installation.
- **Activation Problems:** Verify that your internet connection and license key are functioning properly. If the problem persists, please contact Corel support.
- **Missing Features**: Review the custom installation options to guarantee that all desired components are implemented.

Navigating the User Interface

The interface of CorelDRAW is intended to improve user productivity by facilitating access to essential **tools** and **properties**. The Welcome Screen is displayed upon application activation, providing users with access to recent projects, tutorials, and updates on **what's new**. The primary workspace is comprised of a variety of windows and bars, such as the **Property Bar**, **Status Bar,** and **Standard Toolbar**. Each of these components offers immediate access to a variety of functions that are specifically designed for the current task.

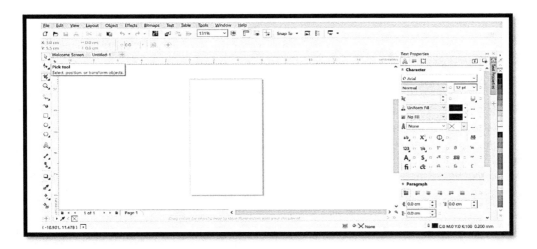

1. The current file's name and path are displayed in the Title Bar.
2. The drop-down menus of the program can be accessed by clicking on the item's name in the Menu Bar.
3. The Status Line displays the current mode and information regarding the object that is currently selected.
4. The Toolbox is a collection of fundamental drawing and manipulation tools that are employed to generate drawings. The mouse pointer is transformed into the intended tool by clicking on the icon.
5. The Tool fly-out menus offer access to a variety of supplementary options that are revealed upon clicking on their icons.
6. Rulers are employed to accurately measure an object on the page.
7. The Work Area and Page are utilized to draw and manipulate objects. This is a display of your illustration that is "What You See Is What You Get" (WYSIWYG). The page settings, which can be accessed through the File menu, will determine the orientation and extent of the area within the page boundary.
8. Object handles are small boxes that appear on the borders of the object that is presently selected. Handles can be employed to extend and size an object.
9. A roll-up menu is a selection box that provides access to the options for the Text tool and specific special effects in the work area without the need to use the standard menu bar. One of the menus is displayed in its entirety, while the other is reduced to a small bar by selecting the **Minimize** option located at the upper right corner.
10. The On-Screen Palette is a band of predefined colors and grayscale tones that can be clicked on to rapidly establish a solid fill.
11. The Page Counter is a feature that is only visible when the drawings file contains more than one page and is utilized to navigate from one page to another.
12. The area displayed in the active window is repositioned using Windows Scroll Bars.

Menus

Drop-Down Menus

Ten drop-down menus are situated above the status bar or the ruler in CorelDRAW. Drawing commands and special effects are accessible through the Edit, Effects, Text, and Arrange menus. The File, Layout, and View menus are utilized to import files generated by other applications, add or modify pages, and personalize CorelDRAW's functionality. Additionally, they are employed to open and save drawings. The Tools window provides the user with additional functionality if required. Shifting and viewing additional files within the program is possible through the Window menu. The online assistance features are accessible through the assistance menu. To access a menu, you can either click on its name or utilize a keyboard shortcut. Shortcuts are activated by pressing the key that corresponds to the letter underlined in the menu's name while holding down the Alt key. To select an option after the menu has been opened, strike the letter that is underlined, but do not hold down the Alt key.

Fly-Out Menus

Fly-out menus are activated by selecting icons in the Toolbox. To activate an option or access its dialog box, simply click on it when the menu is visible.

Dialog Boxes

Dialog panels are employed to configure numerous options. This enables CorelDRAW to maintain a clean interface while still providing fast access to settings and commands. New users can find the number of variations to be complex; however, with a little practice, they will become second nature.

Roll-up Menus

Roll-up menus are unique menus that can be left on the screen while you are working and are utilized to modify objects without the need to use the standard dialog windows. They resemble miniature toolboxes. CorelDRAW provides a variety of methods for executing the majority of commands. The task can be accomplished using the mouse, special keys, keyboard shortcuts, roll-up menu, or dialog window. Select the approach that is most effective for you, but remain receptive to modifying your approach as your abilities develop. Searching for hot keys and shortcuts for the commands that are used most frequently can significantly expedite your workflow.

Exploring the Toolbox

The **Toolbox**, a comprehensive collection of **Drawing Tools**, **Text Tools**, and **Shaping Tools**, is the foundation of CorelDRAW's functionality. The Toolbox is typically located on the left side of the screen and contains essential tools such as the Pick Tool, which is used to select and position objects, and the Shape Tool, which enables the manipulation of object nodes and curves. The Property Bar allows you to modify the properties of each tool in the CorelDRAW Toolbox to meet the unique requirements of your project.

This is where you will locate the Toolbox.

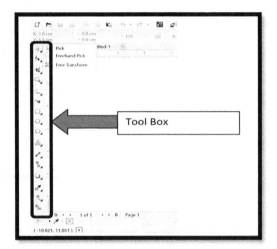

Additionally, there is a Tool Drop down Menu in the Menu bar; however, the ToolBox encompasses all of the important ones. Upon selecting each tool, its drop-down options will be displayed, and their properties will be displayed individually in the Tool Bar below the Menu Bar. Initially, we should conduct a thorough examination of each tool.

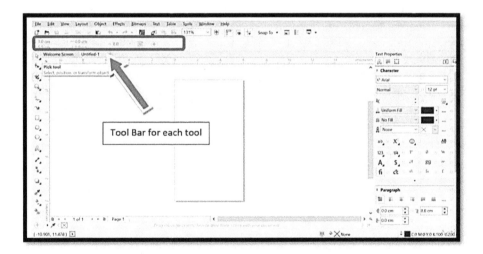

Features of Different Tools in CorelDraw

The following tools play a significant role in CorelDRAW, enhancing the overall experience for graphics designers by improving precision, flexibility, and creative possibilities:

1. **Pick Tool**: The Pick Tool is a fundamental feature that lets users select and modify objects in their workspace. It facilitates repositioning, resizing, rotating, and skewing objects, offering a versatile

way to manipulate elements in a design. Additionally, it supports quick access to other tools, streamlining the design workflow.

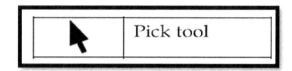

2. **Shape Tool**: The Shape Tool is indispensable for refining and adjusting object angles and outlines. Its flexibility allows users to edit shapes with precision.

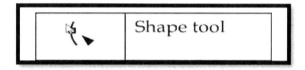

- o **Smudge Brush**: This brush blends and blurs areas of an image by dragging it along the desired path. It's particularly effective for creating smooth transitions and adding textured effects to edges like shorelines, giving the design a dynamic and artistic appeal.
- o **Roughen Brush**: This brush imparts a rugged, hand-drawn effect by altering the outlines of shapes. It is especially useful for creating organic, textured edges, adding a unique and creative touch to designs.

3. **Free Transform Tools**: Free Transform Tools allow users to manipulate image objects in multiple ways. They can rotate objects freely or at specific angles, resize them to match exact dimensions, and reshape them to align with design needs. This set of tools is essential for achieving both creative and technical precision.

4. **Crop Tool**: The Crop Tool is designed for removing unwanted areas of an image with high accuracy. It is perfect for focusing on key elements or refining composition by trimming away distractions. The tool includes several additional features:

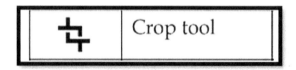

- o **Virtual Segment Delete Tool**: This tool is ideal for cleaning up designs by selectively removing intersecting or overlapping parts of objects, ensuring a clean and organized appearance.
- o **Erase Tool**: By defining specific areas to remove, the Erase Tool helps users refine their designs further. It allows for precise elimination of unwanted elements, ensuring a polished and professional result.

5. **Zoom Tool**: The Zoom Tool is crucial for conducting a detailed examination of objects by adjusting the magnification level. It offers additional functionality through its sub-tool:

- o **Hand Tool**: This tool allows users to move across the canvas effortlessly, especially when working on magnified views. It preserves the original layout and ensures easy navigation without disrupting the composition. This combination of zoom and movement is essential for intricate design work.

6. **Curve Tools**: Curve Tools provide flexibility in creating and modifying the shapes, angles, and dimensions of images. **Below is a detailed explanation of some of the most frequently used Curve Tools in CorelDRAW:**

- **Freehand Tool**: This tool allows users to draw curves and lines directly using a mouse or similar input device. It's ideal for creating organic, hand-drawn shapes that give a natural, sketch-like appearance to designs.

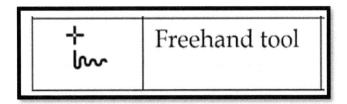

- **Bezier Tool**: The Bezier Tool is used to craft precise curves by creating single line segments between points. It gives designers control over complex shapes by placing nodes and adjusting their control handles, ensuring smooth and seamless paths.
- **Pen Tool**: This tool is designed for creating intricate curves by manually placing and adjusting nodes, offering precise control over shapes and trajectories.
- **Three-Point Curve Tool**: This tool simplifies the creation of curves by defining three points: a start point, an end point, and a midpoint to adjust the arc. It ensures accuracy in designing curves with specific measurements.
- **Poly-line Tool**: The Poly-line Tool combines lines and curves into a connected sequence. It allows for quick creation of geometrical shapes, with the option to preview and adjust segments on the go.
- **Dimension Tool**: Ideal for technical and architectural drawings, this tool allows for precise placement of horizontal, vertical, oblique, and angular lines. It includes measurement annotations, making it a go-to for layouts that demand high precision.
- **Interactive Connector Tool**: Designed for creating flowcharts and diagrams, this tool draws lines that connect objects, visually representing relationships between elements.

7. **Artistic Media Tool**: The Artistic Media Tool provides creative brush effects that include options like sprayers, calligraphy, and pressure-sensitive strokes. It helps designers incorporate artistic elements into their projects, ranging from bold brush strokes to intricate patterns. This tool adds a unique, stylized look to designs, allowing users to transform ordinary lines into eye-catching effects effortlessly.

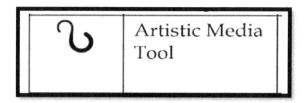

8. **Rectangle Tool**: The Rectangle Tool generates geometric shapes like squares and rectangles. It is frequently used to create frames, boxes, or structural elements with precise edges and linear sides. A supplementary tool enhances its utility:
   - **Three-Point Rectangle**: This variant lets users draw rectangles by defining three points: the start point, width, and height. It simplifies the process of creating rectangles aligned at any angle.

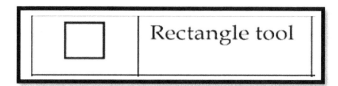

9. **Ellipse Tool**: The Ellipse Tool allows users to create perfect circles and ellipses by manipulating width and height directly on the canvas. For proportional and symmetrical shapes, users can hold down the SHIFT key while resizing, ensuring accurate aspect ratios for precise designs.

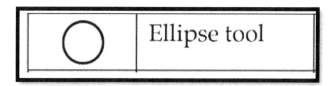

10. **Polygon Tool**: The Polygon Tool creates symmetrical polygons like triangles, pentagons, hexagons, and stars. By specifying the number of sides and adjusting the radius, users can achieve consistent and balanced designs. The tool also supports two star variations:

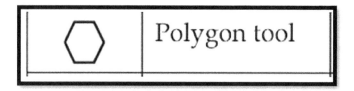

   - **Star Tool**: Used for designing simple stars, such as traditional five-pointed stars, or customizing stars with varying sizes and points by modifying the inner and outer radius.

- **Complex Star Tool**: This tool allows for advanced customization, enabling users to create intricate star shapes with intersecting angles and deeper indentations.
11. **Basic Shapes Tool**: The Basic Shapes Tool includes a variety of predefined shapes, such as smiley faces, triangles, and hexagrams, which can be used for diagrams, charts, and directional elements. Key options include:

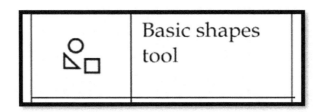

- **Arrow Shapes**: This feature simplifies creating arrows of various styles, including standard arrowheads and more elaborate designs. It also supports slanted rectangles, which can be adjusted diagonally for added flexibility.
- **Flowchart Shapes**: Designed for constructing flowcharts, this option includes specialized shapes for representing processes, decisions, connectors, and start or end points, making it an essential tool for visual communication.
12. **Text and Table Tool**: The Text and Table Tool in CorelDRAW makes it easy to integrate text and tables into your designs.
    - **Table Tool**: This feature helps users create and edit tables with customizable rows and columns. It allows for adding, deleting, and formatting cells, resizing rows and columns, and applying various formatting styles to enhance visual presentation.
    - **Text Tool**: The Text Tool enables users to generate paragraphs and text elements, which can be seamlessly incorporated into designs. It supports features like font selection, alignment adjustments, and text styling, making it suitable for creating everything from headlines to detailed body text.

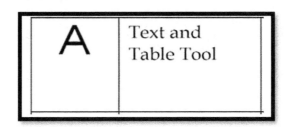

13. **Dimension Tools**: CorelDRAW includes a range of dimension tools that allow users to draw precise lines and add annotations with specific measurements. These tools are particularly useful in technical drawings, architectural plans, and other detailed projects. Frequently used dimension tools include:
    - **Horizontal or Vertical Dimension Tool**: This tool creates dimension lines aligned with the horizontal or vertical measurements of objects. It helps clearly define the length or height of components in a design.

- **Three-Point Callout Tool**: This tool adds callouts to highlight essential elements within a drawing. By attaching labels or annotations, it ensures critical details are easily identified and referenced in future revisions or presentations.

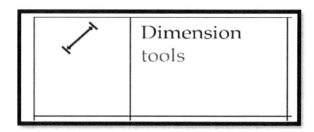

14. **Connector Tools**: Connector Tools in CorelDRAW are used to establish relationships between objects by drawing various types of connecting lines. These tools enhance visual flow and help communicate sequences and associations effectively. Commonly used connector tools include:
    - **Right-Angle Connector Tool**: This tool draws lines that connect two objects at right angles, creating a clean and structured appearance. It's often used in flowcharts and diagrams.
    - **Edit Anchor Tool**: The Edit Anchor Tool allows users to modify connection points between lines or shapes. This flexibility enables designers to adjust the contour and positioning of connected elements to align with the overall design requirements.

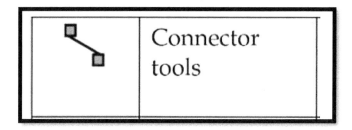

15. **Interactive Tools**: CorelDRAW includes a variety of Interactive Tools that allow users to transform and enhance objects dynamically. These tools provide designers with flexibility and precision for achieving professional results. Below are the key interactive tools and their functionalities:

Interactive Blend	- Creates seamless transitions between two or more objects. - Allows users to define starting and ending shapes, generating intermediate shapes for smooth blending. - Perfect for gradient effects, morphing shapes, and complex transitions
Interactive Distortion	-Creates seamless transitions between two or more objects. - Allows users to define starting and ending shapes, generating intermediate shapes for smooth blending. - Perfect for gradient effects, morphing shapes, and complex transitions

Interactive Distortion	- Applies effects like pull, push, zipper, and twister to objects. - Users can manipulate control points to stretch, warp, or twist objects, creating abstract or surreal designs. - Ideal for adding organic and fluid transformations.
Interactive Mesh	- Adds a mesh-like grid to objects, allowing for detailed manipulation of color and shading. - Control points on the mesh can be adjusted to create smooth tonal transitions and realistic textures. - Excellent for natural textures and subtle shading effects.
Interactive Drop Shadow	- Adds realistic shadow effects to objects for a three-dimensional appearance. - Provides control over shadow position, size, transparency, and softness. - Commonly used to simulate depth and light source effects in designs.
Interactive Fill	- Enables the application of fills such as solid colors, gradients, patterns, and textures to objects. - Users can customize fill properties interactively, adjusting color stops, direction, and transparency for precision. - Enhances designs with versatile visual elements.

These interactive tools allow for creativity and customization, making them invaluable for crafting visually compelling and detailed designs. Whether creating smooth blends, intricate shadows, or organic distortions, these tools offer a wide range of possibilities for designers.

16. **Eyedropper Tool**: The Eyedropper Tool in CorelDRAW is a versatile feature that allows users to sample and replicate the properties of objects within a design. These properties include dimensions, colors, line thickness, and other formatting effects. By using this tool, designers can ensure consistency in styling and formatting across different elements of their projects, streamlining the creative process and maintaining a cohesive appearance.

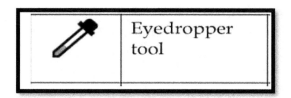

17. **Outline Tool**: The Outline Tool is designed for customizing the appearance of object outlines. With this tool, users can adjust attributes such as outline color, thickness, and style. Accessing the fly-out menu provides further options, allowing for intricate customization. Whether creating bold outlines or subtle borders, this tool offers flexibility to suit various design needs.

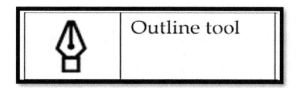

18. **Fill Tool**: The Fill Tool is essential for enhancing the visual appeal of designs by applying different fill effects to objects. It provides options for solid colors, gradients, patterns, and textures, enabling users to create dynamic and engaging visuals. The tool's fly-out menu offers advanced customization options, allowing designers to experiment with fill properties and achieve unique artistic effects tailored to their projects.

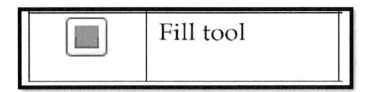

Mastering Basic Operations

An individual must acquire the ability to effectively manage objects, create and manipulate fundamental shapes, utilize guides and grids, and handle text elements to master CorelDRAW.

Working with Basic Shapes

CorelDRAW offers a variety of powerful tools for the creation of basic shapes, including rectangles, ellipses, and polygons. The Rectangle and Ellipse tools are essential for drawing borders or frames. This can be easily accomplished by double-clicking on the corresponding tool icon. The Polygon tool is indispensable for the development of personalized shapes, as it enables the specification of the number of sides for a wide range of designs.

Creating and Managing Objects

A streamlined workflow is contingent upon the effective administration of objects. The Objects docker in CorelDRAW streamlines the process of managing objects by offering convenient access to align and distribute options for precise positioning. The docker can be employed to align multiple objects to a selected boundary or center point, thereby ensuring that the design elements are cohesive. Users can select multiple objects.

Utilizing Guides and Grids

When accuracy is paramount, the utilization of grids and guides guarantees precise alignment and positioning. CorelDRAW's grid system serves as a reference for element placement, while guides—both static and live—provide interactive support for aligning objects as you draw and move them around the canvas. These cues can be used to enhance the accuracy and consistency of objects by attaching them to them.

Manipulating Text

CorelDRAW provides two primary text types: **artistic text** for headlines and brief blasts of text, and **paragraph text** for larger blocks. To add and format text, select the Text tool and click on the canvas. The formatting options are extensive, enabling the modification of font, size, style, and alignment. The design of communicative and visually enticing graphics is significantly influenced by **Text formatting**.

Advanced Design Techniques

Users can generate sophisticated graphics with a professional appearance by mastering advanced design techniques in CorelDRAW. This section explores techniques for improving designs by manipulating color, contours, fills, shapes, and effects.

Utilizing Color Effectively

It is essential to select the appropriate color palette for a design. Users of CorelDRAW should implement color theory to attain visual equilibrium and evoke emotions. The overall impact of the artwork can be improved by establishing cohesive and enticing color palettes with the assistance of tools like the Color Harmonies function.

Working With Outlines and Fills

Vector illustrations are constructed from the foundation of outlines and fills. To enhance the character of the graphics, users can modify the outline properties, such as the weight and dash style. Additionally, they can incorporate a variety of fill options, such as gradient and pattern fills, to add dimension and texture. Designers can generate gradients that are more intricate and realistic by employing the Interactive Fill Tool.

Designing Business Cards and Brochures

A graphic designer working on business cards and brochures in CorelDRAW can start by choosing a suitable template or creating a custom layout from scratch. For business cards, the focus should be on clear readability and prominently displaying contact details, ensuring the essential information stands out. On the other hand, brochures allow for more detailed content and visuals, providing space to communicate key messages effectively. CorelDRAW's layout tools help designers achieve precise alignment and positioning of elements, ensuring the final design is both visually appealing and practical. By balancing functionality with aesthetics, designers can create professional business cards and brochures that effectively represent their brand or message.

- **Business Cards:** A standard size of 3.5" x 2" is typically employed. Ensure that the text is centered and that the margins are sufficient by adhering to the guidelines.
- **Brochures:** Pay close attention to the fold lines and sections. Six panels will be required to be designed separately for Tri-fold brochures.

Enhanced Text Handling

An undertaking can be significantly improved through the use of effective typography. CorelDRAW's text tools assist designers in the resizing of text, the modification of typefaces, and the refinement of spacing. The process is simplified by the alterations docker, which allows designers to efficiently experiment with various typographic settings. Designers must comprehend the impact of typography on the viewer's perception and intelligibility.

- **Key Actions:**
  - **Text Resize:** To maintain proportion, hold down the 'Shift' key while dragging.
  - **Typography Adjustments:** Employ the adjustments docker to adjust the kerning, leading, and tracking.

Understanding Page Layout

An effective comprehension of page layout is essential for a graphic designer who is engaged in any typographical or layout project. CorelDRAW's layout tools assist users in the organization of content in a cohesive manner, adhering to professional standards that contribute to a refined and effective design. It is imperative to take into account the overall flow of content, spacing, and margins to create a layout that is both visually appealing and user-friendly.

- **Layout Tips:**
  - **Consistency:** Ensure that the margins and spacing are consistent to achieve a cohesive appearance.
  - **Flow:** Guarantee that the content is organized in a manner that facilitates the reader's progression through the material.

Designers can execute professional layouts and sophisticated typography with precision and creativity by utilizing the potent tools in CorelDRAW.

Optimizing CorelDRAW Workflows

To enhance productivity in CorelDRAW, it is recommended that users utilize the built-in tools and features that facilitate the design process. These include the utilization of templates, the implementation of automation, and the improvement of collaboration, all of which simplify and optimize the delivery of high-quality work.

Streamlining Projects with Templates

CorelDRAW templates are indispensable assets for optimizing design processes. Designers ensure consistency across comparable projects by utilizing templates, which saves time. For example, a brochure layout template can establish a consistent design, margins, and dimensions for a variety of print materials. One can considerably reduce the setup time for future designs by following a **step-by-step** guide to establish a desired project as a template and save it for reuse. To create a custom template, simply follow the instructions.

Leveraging Automation Features

CorelDRAW's automation feature enables users to execute repetitive duties with greater efficiency and reduced error rates. **Variable data printing** is facilitated by features such as **Print Merge**, which merges individual entries from a data source into a static design. This feature is particularly useful for the creation of personalized certificates or address labels. Furthermore, **macros** can be generated or installed to implement intricate or multi-step operations with the press of a button, thereby enhancing efficiency.

Enhancing Collaboration

Productivity is enhanced through the simplification of communication and feedback and the enhancement of collaboration. CorelDRAW provides collaboration capabilities that facilitate seamless teamwork. The **Sync and Share** function enables users to synchronize and update symbols across various projects, thereby guaranteeing that all team members have access to the most recent versions. This real-time sharing of assets across workspaces facilitates the acceleration of iterative processes and the preservation of consistency.

CHAPTER TWO

GETTING STARTED

Setting Up Your Workspace

To guarantee a personalized, efficient, and seamless design experience, it is essential to configure your workspace in CorelDRAW 2025. Customizing the workspace allows you to customize the tools, panels, and shortcuts to suit your workflow, regardless of whether you are a beginner or a professional designer.

Understanding the CorelDRAW Workspace

The workspace is the environment in which you interact with CorelDRAW's tools, menus, and design elements. The following are the primary components:

1. **Menu Bar:** Offers access to a variety of menus, including file, edit, and view.
2. **Toolbar:** A collection of symbols that provide immediate access to frequently utilized tools and functions.
3. **Toolbox:** Comprises the primary design tools, including the Pick, Shape, and Text tools.
4. **Property Bar:** Presents context-sensitive options for the specified object or tool.
5. **Docker Panels:** Side panels that facilitate the management of layers, text, objects, and other components.
6. **Color Palette:** Enables the application of colors to text and objects.
7. **Rulers, Grids, and Guidelines:** Facilitate precise alignment and layout.
8. **Status Bar:** Displays information about the selected object or tool.
9. **Drawing Page:** The primary canvas on which you develop your design.

1. **Selecting a Workspace Layout**

CorelDRAW 2025 provides pre-defined workspace configurations to accommodate a variety of user requirements:

- **Default Workspace:** A balanced layout designed for common use.
- **Lite Workspace:** A simplified version of the standard workspace, featuring fewer tools and panels to accommodate novice users.
- **Illustrator Workspace:** Concentrated on vector illustration tools.
- **Page Layouts Workspace:** A page layout workspace that is optimized for typography and multi-page documents.
- **Custom Workspace:** Completely customized to accommodate your preferences.

Switching or selecting a workspace:

- Navigate to **Window, and then Workspace**.
- Click on **New Workspace** to establish your workspace or select a predefined workspace.
  1. **Customizing Toolbars and Panels**
- **Rearranging Toolbars:**
  - Reposition toolbars by dragging and dropping them.
  - To access options such as concealing, floating, or anchoring, right-click on a toolbar.
- **Adding/Removing Tools:**
  - Proceed to the **Tools** menu, select **Options**, and then select **Customization**.
  - Access the **Commands tab**, locate the desired tool, and drag it to the toolbar.

- **Dockers (Side Panels):**
  - Open frequently used dockers, including **Object Manager, Layers**, and **Text**, by selecting **Window > Dockers**.
  - Drag dockers to position them on the left or right side of the workspace.
  2. **Setting Up Color Palettes**
- **Default Color Palette:**
  - A default palette that is suitable for the majority of projects is loaded by CorelDRAW.
  - To modify the palette, navigate to **Window > Color Palettes > Palette Manager**.
- **Custom Palettes:**
  - To generate a personalized palette, navigate to **Window > Color Palettes > Create Palette.**
  - Add colors to your custom pallet by dragging them from the color selector.
- **Pantone and CMYK Palettes:**
  - To access the Pantone or CMYK palettes for professional printing, navigate to **Window > Color Palettes**.
  3. **Configuring Rulers, Grids, and Guidelines**
- **Rulers**:
  - Enable rulers from **View > Rulers**.
  - Adjust units (e.g., inches, pixels, and millimeters) by right-clicking on the ruler.
- **Grids**:
  - Activate grids via **View > Grid**.
  - Customize grid spacing under **Layout > Document Settings > Grid**.
- **Guidelines**:
  - Drag guidelines from the rulers onto the canvas.
  - Adjust guideline properties under **View > Guidelines Setup**.
  4. **Customizing Keyboard Shortcuts**

Keyboard shortcuts can significantly speed up your workflow. To customize:
- Go to **Tools > Options > Customization**.
- Select **Commands** and click **Shortcut Keys**.
- Assign or modify shortcuts for frequently used tools and actions.
  5. **Saving Your Workspace**

To preserve your customizations for future use:
- Go to **Tools > Save Settings as Default**.
- Alternatively, export your workspace via **Tools > Options > Workspace > Export Workspace**.
- Save the file for backup or to transfer to another machine.

Tips for Efficient Workspace Setup

- **Employ Dual Monitors:** For improved organization, extend dockers and toolbars to a second screen.
- **Enable Snap Features:** Utilize Snap to Objects and Snap to Guidelines to ensure precise alignment.
- **Adjust Zoom and Pan:** Customize the mouse wheel behavior by navigating to **Tools > Options > Display.**

Customizing Toolbars and Shortcuts

Customizing toolbars and shortcuts in CorelDRAW 2025 is a critical step in streamlining your productivity and ensuring that the tools you use most frequently are easily accessible. The interface of CorelDRAW is highly adaptable, allowing users to adjust toolbars, alter their position, add or remove commands, and designate shortcuts to improve efficiency and usability. To begin customizing the toolbar, navigate to the primary menu and select the toolbar customization options. Customization can be accessed by navigating to **Tools > Options**. This menu provides a comprehensive array of options for customizing the interface. The Commands menu in CorelDRAW provides a categorized inventory of all tools and commands. For instance, if you frequently employ the Shape tool or Alignment options, you can easily transfer them from the Commands list onto an existing toolbar or construct a new custom toolbar to accommodate them. The process of relocating toolbars within the workspace is equally straightforward. Toolbars can be positioned at the interface's top, bottom, or sides. Additionally, it is possible to make them float by selecting and dragging them into the workspace. This feature is particularly advantageous when working on a project that necessitates a particular set of tools to be readily accessible. To further customize an existing toolbar, right-click on it and select **Customize Toolbar**. This feature enables you to rearrange, rename, or even delete specific elements. CorelDRAW offers a comprehensive system for assigning and managing shortcuts. Assigning presets can significantly expedite the design process if you frequently employ particular tools. The Shortcut Keys option is available in the customization menu. From this point, locate the tool or command to which you wish to designate a shortcut, click on it, and strike the desired key combination. CorelDRAW will notify you if the shortcut is already in use, enabling you to determine whether to override it or select an alternative combination. For example, you could designate Ctrl+Shift+R to rapidly access the Rectangle tool or Alt+T to toggle the Text tool. It is not solely about convenience when it comes to customizing toolbars and shortcuts; it is also about establishing a workspace that is intuitive to you. Reducing repetitive motions, minimizing menu diving, and increasing creativity can be achieved by investing time in customizing these features. The versatility of CorelDRAW guarantees that you can always revisit and modify these settings to align with your workflow as your design requirements change.

Understanding CorelDRAW File Formats

CorelDRAW is adaptable to a diverse array of industries, including graphic design, publishing, and web development, due to its support for a wide range of file formats. Knowing when and how to employ each format can improve the quality of your final output and streamline your workflow.

CorelDRAW's Native File Format: CDR

CDR is the default file format for CorelDRAW. Projects and all design elements, such as vector graphics, text, colors, and effects, are saved in this format by default. The CDR format is exclusive to CorelDRAW, which guarantees that every aspect of your design is preserved in its original state. It is especially beneficial when working on multi-layered projects or when you wish to save a design for future modification. It is frequently necessary to export or convert CDR files to a more conventional format for sharing or printing, as they are not universally supported by other software.

Importing and Exporting Files

CorelDRAW is exceptionally adaptable, as it can import and export a wide range of file formats, facilitating seamless collaboration and use across multiple platforms. For instance, it is feasible to integrate a Photoshop PSD file to improve a raster-based design or to export a design as a PDF for publishing. This adaptability guarantees that CorelDRAW can be seamlessly integrated into a diverse array of workflows, regardless of whether other team members are employing distinct software.

Commonly Used File Formats in CorelDRAW

1. **AI (Adobe Illustrator):** The AI format, which is frequently employed in vector-based design, is supported by CorelDRAW. This compatibility is indispensable when working with designers who employ Adobe Illustrator. CorelDRAW is capable of importing and exporting AI files; however, certain advanced Illustrator features cannot be completely transferred.
2. **PDF (Portable Document Format):** The PDF format is frequently employed to share and reproduce designs. CorelDRAW's export options enable you to personalize PDFs for specific applications, including the creation of web-ready documents, high-quality prints, or reduced file sizes for email. It is one of the most adaptable formats for guaranteeing that your design appears uniform across various devices.
3. **EPS (Encapsulated PostScript):** EPS is an additional vector format that is frequently employed in professional publishing and printing. It is excellent for logos and designs that are intended for large-format printing because it maintains vector graphics, text, and images in a scalable format.
4. **SVG (Scalable Vector Graphics):** The majority of contemporary browsers support SVG, a web-friendly vector format. CorelDRAW is an exceptional tool for web developers who require scalable illustrations for online applications or websites due to its capacity to export designs as SVG files.
5. **PNG (Portable Network Graphics):** PNG is the preferred format for high-quality images with transparent backgrounds in raster-based designs. CorelDRAW enables the exportation of designs as PNG files with transparent layers and customizable resolutions, which is especially beneficial for web design and branding.
6. **JPG/JPEG (Joint Photographic Experts Group):** The JPG format is frequently employed for raster-based and photographic images. Although transparency is not supported, its compressed nature renders it appropriate for projects that prioritize file size. CorelDRAW provides the ability to regulate compression levels, thereby harmonizing file size and quality.
7. **DXF/DWG (AutoCAD Formats):** DXF and DWG files are standard formats in engineering and architectural design, and CorelDRAW supports them. This compatibility enables the exchange of files with CAD software users and the use of technical illustrations.
8. **PSD (Photoshop):** CorelDRAW's capacity to import PSD files enables you to integrate raster images generated in Photoshop into your designs. This is especially beneficial for mixed-media projects that incorporate both vector and raster components.
9. **TIFF (Tagged Image File Format):** In professional printing workflows, TIFF is particularly well-suited for high-quality raster images. CorelDRAW facilitates the import and export of TIFF files, guaranteeing that the design and printing processes are executed without any degradation in quality.

Special Formats in CorelDRAW

1. **CorelDRAW Template Files (CDT):** If you commonly generate comparable designs, you can save them as CDT files. These templates maintain the layout, color palettes, and design elements, enabling you to commence new projects with a consistent foundation.
2. **CorelDRAW Symbol Library (CSL):** Reusable symbols and elements are stored in the CSL format. This is especially beneficial in the context of branding and packaging design, where the consistent use of logos and iconography is essential.
3. **CorelDRAW Palette Files (CPL):** Custom color palettes can be stored in CPL format. This guarantees that your designs comply with particular trademark guidelines or color palettes.
4. **Animation Formats:** CorelDRAW can export designs to formats such as SWF and GIF for rudimentary animation purposes, which is beneficial for multimedia projects and web design.

When to Use Specific Formats

The selection of a format is contingent upon the objective of your endeavor. CDR or AI files are the optimal choice for designs that can be edited. PDF is the most dependable option for communicating with clients or preparing for printing. SVG or PNG guarantees transparency and scalability for web applications. By comprehending the advantages of each format, you can make well-informed decisions throughout the design process.

How to Set Up Your CorelDRAW Document

Creating a New Document

CorelDRAW offers a variety of methods for generating a new document:
- Select **File** and then **New**.
- Select the **New Document** icon located on the standard toolbar.
- Press the **Ctrl + N** key on your keyboard.
- Select the **New Document** plus sign option located on the **Get Started menu** of the Welcome Screen.

In the New Document dialog box, you can enter your custom settings or choose from a preset.

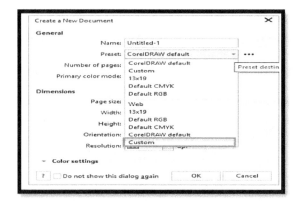

- Select the Web preset if you are composing for the web. The resolution will be set to 150 dpi, and the document units of measure will be converted to pixels automatically.
- The Default RGB configuration can be selected if you are producing for laser engraving or sublimation.
- The Default CMYK preset can be selected if you are engaged in the production of offset printing artwork.

It is also possible to develop a personalized document configuration and subsequently save it as a preset for future use. For instance, 13" x 19" is a typical page size for a large printer. Therefore, we will establish this setting and save it as a preset.

- Select the **Custom** preset.
- Convert the units of measurement to inches.
- In the spaces designated for Width and Height, enter 13 and 19.

Additionally, you have the option to specify the document name, number of pages, principal color mode, and resolution, if required.

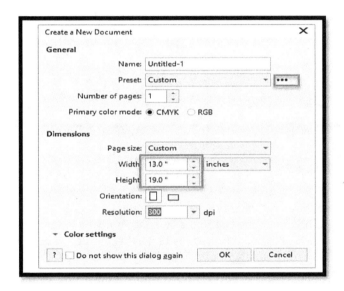

Next, select **Save Preset** by clicking on the three dots located next to the **Preset** dropdown selection. Please enter your name and select **OK.** This new preset will be accessible the next time you initiate a new document. After the settings have been entered, select **OK** to generate the new document. Note that all document settings can be modified within the document by accessing the **Layout menu** and the **Property bar**.

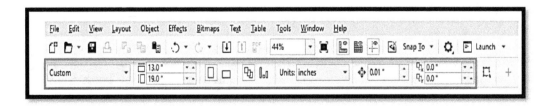

You can also modify the document settings by double-clicking on the grey shadow located at the right and bottom of your CorelDRAW document. This will initiate the Open Document Options window.

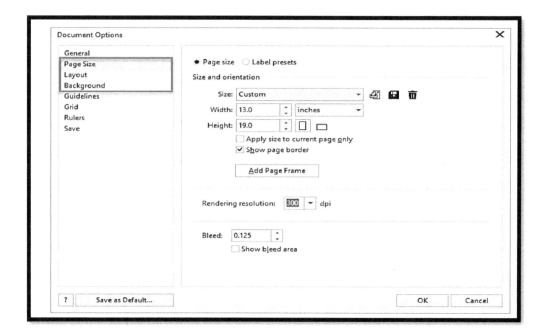

Multiple Page Sizes

Did you know that a CorelDRAW document can contain multiple pages of varying sizes and orientations? The sample exercise file consists of three pages: the first page is 8.5 x 11" and is designated for a sign, the second page is a business card, and the third page is 13 x 19" and is designated for t-shirt artwork. If you require your document to have a variety of page sizes, you will locate a setting in the Property tab that allows you to apply the page size to all pages in the document or the current page only.

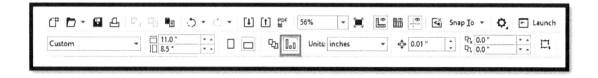

Setting the Duplicate Distance

The distance between the original object and the replicated object is known as the duplicate distance. The default values are 25 and .25; however, some users prefer to set the values to 0:0. This can be beneficial when generating multiple outlines on text or shapes, as the objects are positioned directly on top of one another when duplicated.

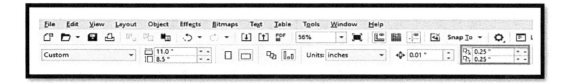

Note: The duplicate distance setting is only visible in the Property tab when there is no selection in the document.

Try it out on the first page of the exercise file:
- Set the duplicate distance to 0:0.
- While maintaining the **Shift** key, select each of the five miniature cupcakes.
- To replicate, select **Edit > replicate** or press **Ctrl + D**.
- The duplicated group of objects will be situated directly above the original objects. Begin dragging to the left or right, and then press and hold the **Ctrl** key. This will ensure that the duplicate objects are in exact alignment with the originals.

Objects On and Off the Page

Another critical aspect of document formatting and printing is that any content that is not on the page or the desktop will not be printed. For instance, ensure that the object or text is located on the page, rather than in the desktop or the document's work area when manually adding registration marks or tags to identify colors or separations.

Units of Measure

When creating a new document, you have the option to select the units of measure for your document in the New Document window. However, you can also modify the units of measure on the property bar. The units of measure set are only visible on the property bar when nothing is selected, as is the case with the duplicate distance setting.

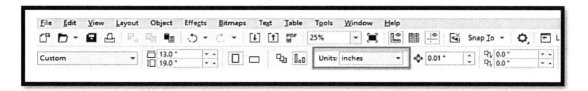

Background Page Color

Adding a background color to your page is a beneficial tip when creating art. The default background of a CorelDRAW document is white. Consequently, white shapes or objects in your artwork can be difficult to discern. **There are two methods for incorporating a background page color into your document:**

1. Utilize the document options to incorporate the background page color:
   - To access the Document Options window, double-click on the shadow of the page or navigate to **Layout > Document Options.**

- Choose **Background** from the left-hand column.
- Select **Solid** and then utilize the color palette from the **Navigation** menu to determine a hue.
- Uncheck the **Print and export background** option.

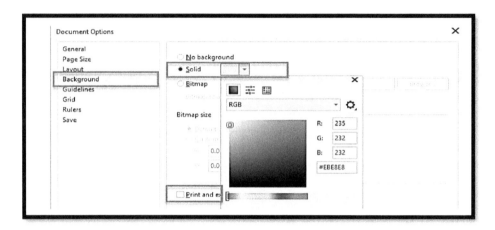

It is important to note that this setting is implemented on all pages of your document.

2. Utilize the **Rectangle** tool to incorporate a background color into the page:
   - Verify that no options are selected in your document.
   - In the **Tools** toolbar, double-click on the **Rectangle** tool. This will generate a rectangle that is equivalent to the dimensions of your document.
   - To cover the rectangle, select a color from the **color palette**.
   - Select **Lock** by right-clicking on the rectangle. This will prevent the rectangle from moving while you are working on other objects in the document.
   - Anytime, you can right-click and select **Unlock**, and if the rectangle is no longer required, you can delete it.

Turn off Treat as Filled

Do you experience difficulty pressing on objects? In some cases, it may be beneficial to disable Treat as Filled. When no objects are selected, the icon **Treat all objects** as filled is visible in the far right corner of the property bar. It is enabled by default, as evidenced by the white frame that surrounds it. To disable the icon, simply click on it. You can also disable it by navigating to **Tools > Options > Tools**, selecting the **Pick** tool in the left column, and then unchecking the **Treat all objects as filled option.**

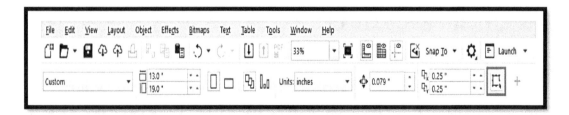

Setting the Zero Point for Rulers

Are you aware that the ruler's 0:0 point can be repositioned within the document? The default position is at the bottom left of the page. However, what if you prefer it to be at the upper left? Drag the ruler intersection (where the rulers intersect at the top left) to the top left corner of the page. **To return the rulers to their default position, simply double-click on the intersection of the rulers.**

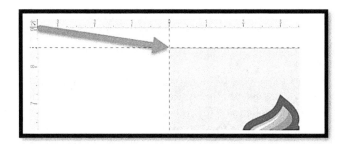

Adding Guidelines

Layout and design are significantly enhanced by guidelines. Initially, navigate to the **View** menu and verify that the **Guidelines** option is selected. There are two methods for adding guidelines. Next, navigate to **Window > Dockers** and select the **Guidelines docker** and the **Object docker.**
1. Navigate to the **Guides** layer on page one of the Objects docker. From the vertical ruler on the left, drag a guide and position it in the desired location on the document. The Object Position box on the property bar allows for precise positioning adjustment
2. **The Guidelines docker can also be used to establish the guidelines:**
   - Assign the **Guideline Type** to either vertical or horizontal, contingent upon the desired type of guideline.
   - Enter the position in the **Guideline Position** box.
   - Select "**Add**."

Saving, Exporting, and Importing Files

The secure storage, effective sharing, and seamless integration of your projects into a variety of operations are all ensured by the fundamental actions of saving, exporting, and importing files in CorelDRAW 2025. Comprehending these processes and their subtleties will enable you to effectively manage your designs while simultaneously ensuring compatibility with other applications and systems.

Saving Files in CorelDRAW

It is essential to save your work to facilitate future revisions and preserve progress. The **CDR** format is the native file type of CorelDRAW, and it preserves all design elements, such as vector data, layers, effects, and typefaces.

Steps to Save Files:
1. **Saving for the First Time:**
    *   Navigate to the **File** menu and select **Save As**.
    *   Select a location on your computer or an external drive.
    *   Ensure that the format is set to **CorelDRAW (*.CDR)** and enter a file name.
    *   Select the **Save** button.
2. **Auto-Save Feature:**
    *   An **Auto-Save** function is incorporated into CorelDRAW to prevent data loss. This feature ensures that your work is saved at predetermined intervals.
    *   To enable or modify it, navigate to **Tools > Options > Workspace > Save** and establish the auto-save interval.
3. **Version Compatibility:**
    *   CorelDRAW enables the saving of files that are compatible with previous versions. Select the desired CorelDRAW version from the Version dropdown in the Save dialog.

The native CDR format is the optimal choice for retaining and editing all project data. Nevertheless, it is frequently necessary to export your design to a different format to share or publish it.

Exporting Files in CorelDRAW

Exporting transforms your design into a format that is suitable for integration into other projects, publishing, or sharing. CorelDRAW accommodates an extensive array of file formats, including PDF, PNG, JPG, SVG, and EPS.

Steps to Export Files

1. **Standard Export:**
    o   Navigate to **File > Export.**
    o   From the navigation menu in the Export dialog, select the file format you wish to export (e.g., PNG, PDF, EPS).
    o   Select a file name and location, and then select **Export**.
2. **Export Settings:**
    o   A preferences dialog will be displayed after a format has been selected. In this section, you can modify settings such as transparency, color mode (RGB or CMYK), and resolution.
    o   For example:
        *   **PNG:** Suitable for web graphics that require transparency.
        *   **PDF:** Ideal for sharing designs with clients or producing high-quality prints.
3. **Batch Export:**
    o   You can export multiple pages or objects from your project as distinct files in a single operation.
    o   Navigate to **File > Export > Export for Batch**, select the objects or pages, and specify the desired format for each.

Exporting guarantees that your designs are available in formats that are appropriate for a variety of applications, including digital use and printing.

Importing Files in CorelDRAW

Importing enables the incorporation of external files into CorelDRAW to modify or integrate them into existing projects. This function is indispensable for collaborating with others or repurposing assets that were generated by other software.

Steps to Import Files

1. **Basic Import**:
   - Go to **File > Import** or press **Ctrl + I**.
   - Navigate to the file you wish to import, select it, and click **Import**.
2. **Placing Imported Files**:
   - After selecting the file, your cursor will change to a placement tool. Click anywhere on the canvas to place the file.
   - Alternatively, drag to define the file's placement and size.
3. **Supported File Formats**:
   - CorelDRAW supports a wide range of formats for importing, including:
     - **AI (Adobe Illustrator)**: Useful for vector graphics.
     - **PSD (Photoshop)**: Allows for raster-based images.
     - **DXF/DWG (AutoCAD)**: Ideal for technical drawings.
4. **Handling Fonts and Links**:
   - If the imported file contains fonts that are not installed on your system, CorelDRAW will prompt you to substitute or install the missing fonts.
   - Linked files (e.g., images) may require you to maintain file paths or embed them during import.

Best Practices for Saving, Exporting, and Importing

1. **Use Layers for Organization**: Organize your design elements on separate layers when storing or exporting. This simplifies the process of modifying and exporting specific components.
2. **Backup Your Work:** Utilize incremental file names (e.g., Design_v1.cdr, Design_v2.cdr) to save multiple versions of your project, particularly during critical stages.
3. **Optimize for Export:** Reduce the size of the file by removing unused objects, concealed layers, or unnecessary elements before exporting.
4. **Understand Format Compatibility:** Ensure that the export format selected is compatible with the recipient's software for collaborative projects. For instance, PDF is universally compatible, whereas AI is exclusive to Adobe Illustrator.
5. **Test Imported Files:** Upon importing a file, verify that all elements, including fonts, layers, and hues, are as anticipated. If required, modify the settings during the import process.

CHAPTER THREE

WORKING WITH SHAPES AND OBJECTS

Creating Basic Shapes

Creating Squares and Rectangles

CorelDRAW allows us to create rectangles and squares. The Rectangle tool can be used to construct a square and rectangle by dragging diagonally or the 3-point rectangle tool can be used to specify the height and breadth. It enables the rapid creation of rectangles with an angle. Additionally, it is feasible to generate rectangles and squares with **scalloped**, **rounded**, and **chamfered corners**. Each corner can be individually modified or these modifications can be applied to each corner. In addition, it is feasible to depict that each corner scale is pertinent to an object. Additionally, we can specify the default corner size to generate rectangles and squares.

To create the rectangle

- Click on the **Rectangle** tool in the toolbar. Drag the tool into the drawing window and create the desired shape.

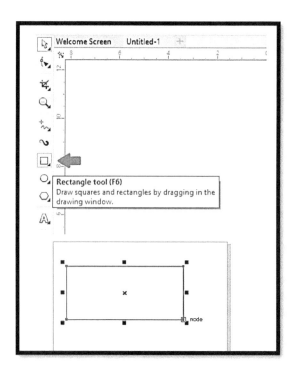

To draw the square

- Press the **Rectangle** tool in the toolbar. Hold down the **Ctrl** button and drag the tool into the drawing window to create the desired shape.

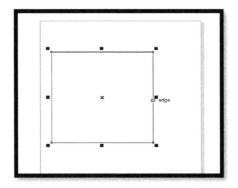

Creating Pie Shapes, Arcs, Circles, and Ellipses

The ellipse tool can be used to construct a circle or ellipse by dragging diagonally, or a 3-point ellipse tool can be used to specify the height and breadth of an ellipse. A 3-point ellipse tool allows us to rapidly generate the ellipse at the desired angle, thereby eradicating the necessity to rotate the ellipse.

To diagonally draw a circle or ellipse by dragging

- Press the **Ellipse** icon in the toolkit. Release the mouse button when the desired ellipse shape is achieved.

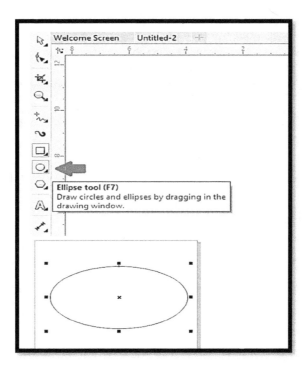

- Press the **Ellipse** icon in the toolkit. Hold down the **Ctrl** button and release the cursor button when you have achieved the desired circle shape.

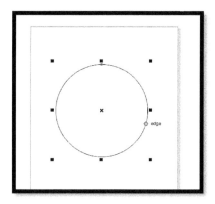

Creating Stars and Polygons

CorelDRAW allows for the creation of two fundamental types of polygons and stars: complex and perfect. Using the fill, the complex star produces intersecting sides and genuine outcomes. The perfect star is characterized by its traditional appearance and the ability to incorporate a fill that covers the entire shape of the star. We can modify the polygons and stars. For instance, we can adjust the number of sides in the polygon or the number of points in the star, and we can enhance the sharpness of the points in the star. Additionally, the Shape tool can be employed to reshape intricate polygons and stars.

To draw the polygons

- Select the **Polygon** tool from the toolbar, drag the mouse cursor within the drawing window, and release it when the desired polygon shape is achieved.

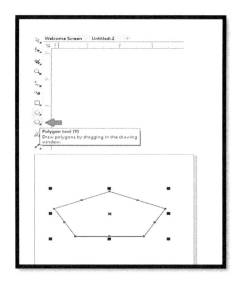

To draw the stars

- Select the **Star** tool from the toolbar, drag the mouse cursor within the drawing window, and release it when the desired polygon shape is achieved.

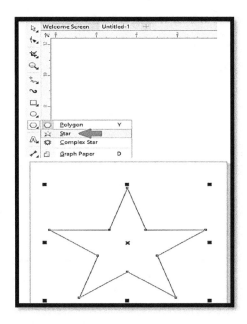

Creating Spirals

We can generate two fundamental spiral types: **symmetrical and logarithmic**. The symmetric spiral disseminates uniformly. Consequently, the distance between each revolution will be equivalent. The logarithmic spiral expands with progressively greater distances throughout the revolution. The rate at which the logarithmic spiral expands can be established.

To draw the spirals

1. Select the **Spiral** icon from the toolbox.

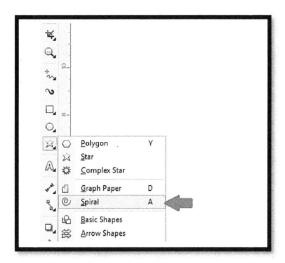

2. The value should be entered into the **Spiral revolutions** box located above the property bar.

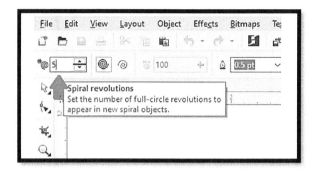

3. Over the property bar, press any button:
- **Symmetric spiral**

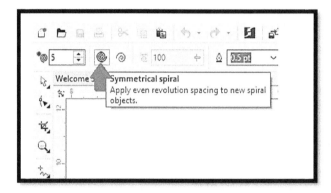

- **Logarithmic spiral**
4. Drag diagonally within the drawing window and release the icon when the desired dimension is achieved.

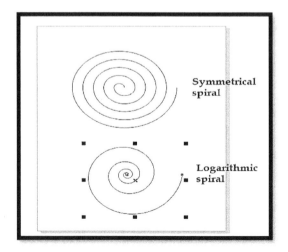

Creating Grids

We can establish the grid and determine the number of columns and rows. The grids are the grouped set of rectangles that we could disassemble. To create a grid from the center outward point, hold down the **Shift button** while dragging. To construct the grid along with the square cells, hold down the **Ctrl button** while dragging.

To draw the grids

1. Press the **Graph paper** button in the toolbox.

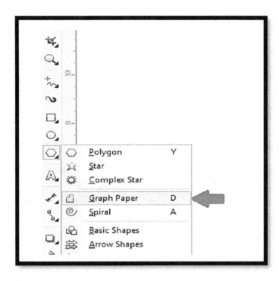

2. The value should be entered into the bottom and upper proportions of the **Columns and Rows** box located on the property bar.

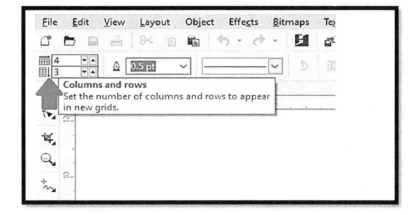

3. Indicate the location where the grid should be displayed.
4. To create the grid, draw diagonally.

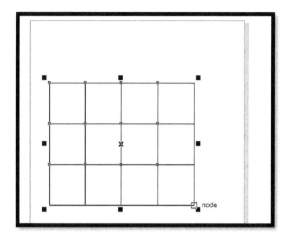

Creating Predefined Shapes

The collection of ideal shapes enables the creation of predefined shapes. Callouts, banners, arrows, and fundamental shapes, such as diamond-shaped **glyphs**, are among the specific shapes. The representation of the geometry can be altered by dragging the glyph. The text can be inserted into the outside or inside of a shape. It may be advantageous to position the label either outside or within a callout or flowchart symbol.

To create the predetermined shapes

1. **Press any of the following options within the toolbox:**
   o **Basic shapes**
   o **Flowchart shapes**
   o **Arrows shapes**
   o **Callout shapes**
   o **Banner shapes**

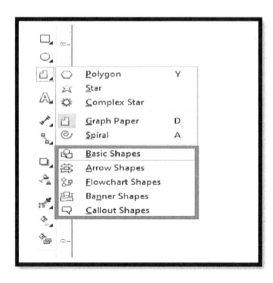

2. Click on any shape in the **Perfect Shapes** selection located above the property bar.

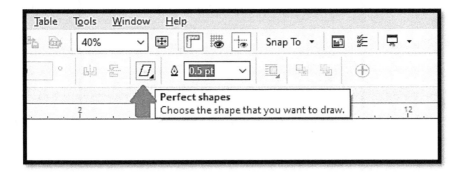

3. When the desired dimension is achieved, release the button and drag the object into the drawing window.

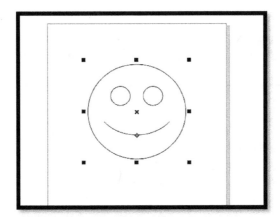

Creating by Applying Shape Recognition

Smart drawing is a tool that can be employed to generate freehand strokes that can be converted and identified as fundamental shapes. Ellipses and rectangles are converted to CorelDRAW objects, parallelograms, and trapezoids are converted to several perfect shapes objects, and arrows, diamonds, squares, triangles, and lines are converted to various curve objects. Smoothing occurs when the elements are not translated into any shape. The ability to edit curves and objects generated through shape recognition is available. We can establish a threshold at which CorelDRAW recognizes the shapes and converts them into specific objects. Additionally, we describe the refining quantity that is applied to curves. The pen stroke can be created at a specific interval of time. We can generate the corrections as we draw. The line style and breadth of the shape that was generated through shape recognition can also be adjusted.

To utilize shape recognition to create lines and shapes

1. Select the **Smart drawing** option from the toolbox.

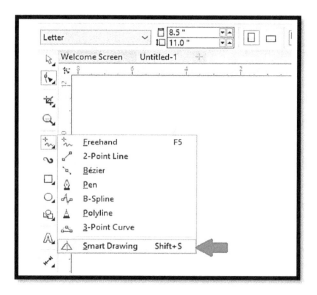

2. Choose a level of recognition by selecting the **Shape recognition level** in the property bar.
3. Choose a smoothing level by selecting the **Smart smoothing level** in the property bar.

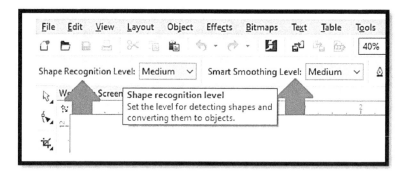

4. Create a line or shape within the drafting window.

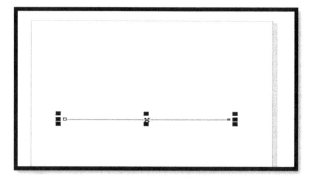

CorelDRAW: Shape Building Basics

1. From Rectangle to Pumpkin

Step 1

Use the **Rectangle Tool** (F6) to create a new document and draw a rectangle. In the Property Bar, you will find options to modify the shape and radius of the corners of the newly drawn rectangle. Select the rectangle. Select **Rounded Corners** and input a value of 2.0" for the **Corner Radius**.

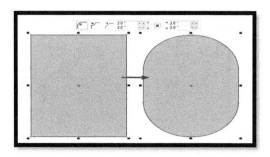

Step 2

To modify the shape's nodes, select the rounded rectangle and select **Convert to Curves (Control-Q)**. Next, use the **Pick Tool** to **scale** the rounded rectangle inward to make it thinner. Finally, use the **Shape Tool (F10)** to adjust the shape's nodes so that the top of the shape is narrower than the bottom (refer to the image below).

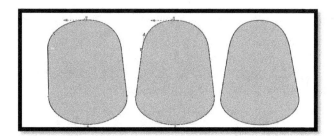

Step 3:

1. **Copy (Control-C)** and **Paste (Control-V)** the rounded rectangle shape. Then, use the Pick Tool to double-click the cloned object to rotate it toward the center of the design.
2. **Copy** and **Paste** the shape on the left and select **Mirror Horizontally** in the Property Bar. Once more, use the **Shape Tool** to modify the nodes of each shape to achieve a more irregular pumpkin appearance.
3. In the Object Manager, position the two side shapes behind the central shape. Paste an additional pumpkin section behind the three objects that have already been drawn. Rotate the pumpkin section to the center, scale it down, and modify the nodes as necessary.
4. I selected a total of six objects. Group your pumpkin shapes together by pressing the **Control-G** key.

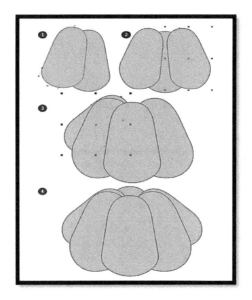

Step 4

In the **Object Manager**, select each section of the pumpkin. In the **Object Properties (Alt-Enter)** window, replace the **Outline** with null and the **Fill** color of each object with a different hue of orange. I selected the following four shades from front to back:

- #FFB02D
- #FF9C1E
- #FF862C
- #FF782C

Copy and Paste the pumpkin group and ungroup the objects by pressing **Control-U**. While all of the objects are still selected, select **Weld** in the **Property Bar**. The welded object will be aligned with its parent item when you copy and paste it. In the **Object Manager**, position the welded object behind the pumpkin group and set the **Outline** to dark orange (#F74A00) at **4.0 pt Weight.**

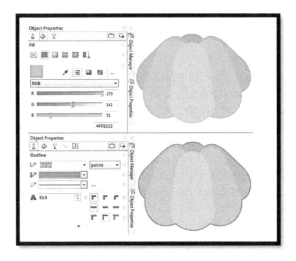

2. From Ellipses to Leaves and a Stem

Step 1

- To create a circle, utilize the **Ellipse Tool (F7)** and maintain a consistent shape by holding down the **Control** key.
- Click on **Convert to Curves** in the Property Bar and utilize the **Shape Tool** to extend the shape into a sideways teardrop by pulling the right node out to the right.
- In the Property Bar, select **Pointy Smear** with the Smear Tool and bring the right side to a point. Adjust the tool's size and pressure to your preference.
- Change to the **Smooth Smear** and meticulously apply it to the leaf shape to create the illusion of a lengthier, wiggling, swaying leaf.
- The extent to which your ellipse assumes an extreme shape is entirely at your discretion. The final shape I achieved is depicted below.

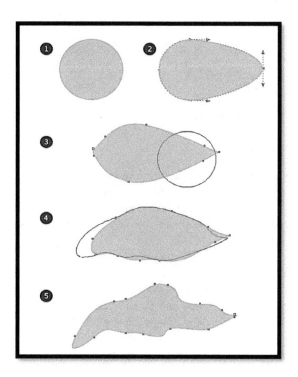

Step 2

- Position the leaf on the pumpkin's top. Adjust the **Scale** and **Rotate** as necessary. **Copy and paste** the leaf to create two copies. In the **Object Properties** docker, add an Outline of **2.0 pt Weight**.
- Draw an ellipse that bisects the first leaf.
- Alter the drawn shape from **Ellipse** to **Arc** in the **Property Bar**. Adjust the **Outline** color to match the leaves' outline color.
- Select the arc and leaf, and then select **Intersect** in the Properties Bar. In the Object Manager, delete the arc object and set the **Outline** of the newly constructed shape to **2.0 pt Weight**.
- **Copy**, **Paste**, and **Rotate** the second leaf. Ensure that the leaf's vein is behind the first leaf in the Object Manager.

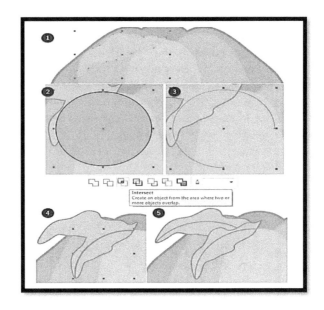

Step 3
Two alternate-shaped tools will be employed to create the stem.

1. Begin by utilizing the **3-Point Ellipse Tool** to create a line that spans the breadth of your stem.
2. Drag the tool upward to construct the ellipse after clicking with your cursor. Maintain a horizontal and relatively narrow shape.
3. Adjust the **Fill** color to brown (#996633).
4. Utilize the **3-Point Rectangle Tool** to drag a line across the ellipse's breadth and then draw a rectangle down to the length of the stem.
5. Set the **Fill** color of both objects to brown and the **Outline** color to null.
6. Copy and paste the ellipse twice and position one at the base of the rectangle. **Weld** the rectangle, the bottom ellipse, and one of the upper ellipses together.

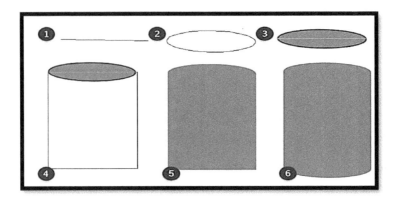

Step 4

- Alter the hue of the welded object to a darker brown (#663300).
- Employ the **Shape Tool** to select the nodes at the base of the stem shape and move them inward.
- Ensure that the bottom is rounded by altering both the nodes and the node handles. Group the two objects together.
- Position the stem beneath the first three sections of the pumpkin (you will probably need to ungroup these objects to do so). Apply a dark brown outline to the primary stem shape with a weight of 2.0–3.0 pts.

Step 5

In the **Toolbox**, there is a multitude of custom shape tools located under the **Polygon Tool (Y).** Select the Spiral Tool (A), set the number of **Spiral Revolutions** to 2, and select **Logarithmic Spiral**. Draw a few spiral shapes and position them close to the stem and leaves.

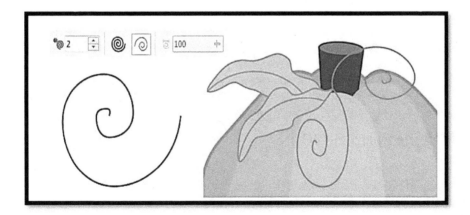

Great Job, You're Done!

We have covered the fundamentals of CorelDRAW, including the **Ellipse Tool, Rectangle Tool, Property Bar, Object Manager, Object Properties, and Smear Tool**. What other objects can you generate using custom shapes and assorted polygons? Please share your Halloween designs, such as pumpkins, in the comment section below.

Advanced Shape Manipulation

Node Editing for Precision

The capacity to modify shapes at the node level is one of CorelDRAW's most sophisticated shape manipulation capabilities. Nodes are responsible for defining the structure of a shape, and their modification provides an unparalleled level of control over its appearance.

1. **Convert to curves:** To initiate advanced editing, select the object and navigate to **Object > Convert to Curves (Ctrl+Q).** This process converts a fundamental geometry into an editable path.
2. **Employing the Shape Tool:** You can manipulate nodes and control points on the object's path using the Shape Tool (F10).
   - **Add or Remove Nodes:** To modify the complexity of the shape, right-click on the path and add or remove nodes.
   - **Move Nodes:** To reshape the object, drag the nodes.
   - **Adjust Curves:** Utilize control handles to adjust the curvature between nodes.
3. **Nodes:** CorelDRAW provides a variety of node types to facilitate precise control:
   - **Cusp Nodes:** Establish transitions between curves that are particularly pointed.
   - **Smooth Nodes:** Guarantee a gradual transition for curves that flow.
   - **Symmetrical Nodes:** Ensure that the handles are balanced to ensure that the curves are uniform.

Shape Merging and Splitting

CorelDRAW offers the ability to consolidate or divide objects, enabling the combination of numerous shapes into a single entity or the division of them into distinct components.

1. **Weld:** The Weld feature is capable of combining two or more contiguous objects to form a single shape. For instance, a teardrop shape can be generated by welding a circle and a rectangle.

2. **Trim:** To remove overlapping sections of objects, employ the Trim tool. In the Property Bar, select the object to be trimmed and the object from which it should be trimmed, and then select the Trim option.
3. **Intersect Tool:** The Intersect tool is particularly advantageous for the development of intricate designs by extracting overlapping regions, as it generates a new shape when two objects intersect.
4. **Simplify Tool:** The Simplify tool optimizes your design by eliminating unnecessary overlapping paths in intricate objects, thereby decreasing the size of the file.

Envelope and Perspective Tools

The Envelope and Perspective tools provide unparalleled adaptability for dynamic shape transformation.
1. **Envelope:** By manipulating the bounding box of objects, the Envelope Tool is capable of reshaping them. This capability is particularly advantageous for the creation of distorted text or objects that adhere to a particular contour.
    o Activate the Envelope Tool from the Toolbox by selecting the object.
    o To dynamically reshape the object, drag the control points of the bounding box.
2. **Perspective:** To create a 3D effect, apply perspective to your designs to simulate depth and dimension. Select the object and navigate to **Effects > Add Perspective**. Drag the corners to modify the perspective.

Shaping Docker

The Shaping Docker serves as a central center for numerous shape manipulation functions, providing a consolidated interface for operations such as welding, pruning, and intersecting.
1. To access the Docker, navigate to **Window > Dockers > Shaping**.
2. Employ it to apply sophisticated operations to multiple shapes simultaneously, thereby saving time on complex projects.

Blending and Contouring Shapes

Blending and contouring are sophisticated techniques that enable the creation of visually striking effects.
1. **Blending:** The Blend Tool enables the creation of a sequence of intermediate shapes between two objects. For instance, the seamless transition between the forms of a circle and a square is achieved by merging the two.
    • Select both objects, activate the **Blend Tool,** and drag from one object to the other.
2. **Contouring:** The Contour Tool is a valuable tool for generating decorative patterns or outlines, as it generates numerous concentric shapes within or outside an object.
    • Activate the **Contour** Tool, select the object, and enter the number of steps and distance in the **Property Bar**.

PowerClips and Shape Effects

PowerClips and Effects provide supplementary methods for improving your designs.
1. **PowerClip:** For example, the PowerClip feature can be employed to embed one object within another. For example, a texture or image can be clipped into a shape.
    • Choose the object to be clipped, navigate to **Effects > PowerClip > Place inside Frame**, and select the target shape.

2. **Effects:** To enhance the depth and complexity of your designs, incorporate artistic effects such as shadows, transparency, or distortions. These options can be accessed via the **Effects** menu.

Combining and Welding Shapes

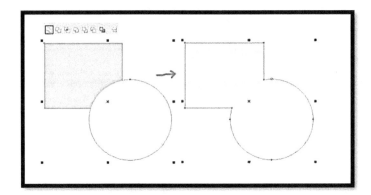

CorelDRAW offers powerful tools like Weld, Trim, Intersect, and Combine, which are essential for combining and modifying shapes to create intricate and unique designs. These features allow designers to transform simple shapes into complex illustrations effortlessly:

- **Weld**: This option lets you merge two or more shapes into one unified shape. It's ideal for creating custom shapes or joining overlapping objects to form seamless designs that would otherwise be difficult to achieve with individual elements.
- **Trim**: The Trim tool enables precise cutting of shapes at their intersections. It's perfect for creating cutouts, removing unwanted sections, or adding intricate details to shapes.
- **Intersect**: By using the Intersect option, you can generate a new shape from the overlapping areas of multiple objects. This feature is excellent for crafting detailed patterns and designs with clean intersections.
- **Combine**: The Combine tool merges shapes without removing overlapping parts. This allows you to maintain the appearance of individual elements while treating them as a single object, making it easier to create visually compelling designs that retain the characteristics of each shape.

To use these features, select the shapes you want to modify, navigate to the Shape menu, and choose the desired option. Experiment with different combinations and adjustments to refine your designs and achieve the exact look you want. These tools offer flexibility and precision, enabling you to create standout graphics with ease.

Understanding Weld Option in CorelDRAW

The Weld option in CorelDRAW is a powerful feature that allows users to combine two or more objects into a single, unified shape. This tool is particularly useful for creating cohesive designs, intricate shapes, and custom elements. Mastering the Weld option can significantly expand your design possibilities within CorelDRAW.

Key Benefits of the Weld Option

- **Seamless Merging**: It fuses overlapping areas of selected objects, resulting in a single shape with no overlapping lines or gaps.
- **Typography Customization**: The Weld tool is especially effective for designing custom typography, enabling you to merge overlapping letterforms or shapes into a single cohesive design.

Steps to Use the Weld Option

1. **Create Objects**: Draw or place the shapes you wish to merge.
2. **Select Objects**: Highlight all the objects you want to weld by dragging your mouse over them or holding down the Shift key while clicking each object.
3. **Access the Weld Option**: Go to the **Arrange menu** and select **Weld**. Alternatively, use the Weld button in the property bar (if available).
4. **Merge Shapes**: The selected objects will merge into a single, unified object.

Important Considerations

- **Irreversible Changes**: Once objects are welded, their individual components cannot be edited separately. If you need to make adjustments, you'll need to undo the weld and restart the process.
- **Experimentation**: Test different object combinations to see how the Weld tool affects your designs. This can help you discover creative ways to simplify complex designs or develop unique shapes.

The Weld option is a valuable tool for simplifying intricate designs and creating visually striking elements in CorelDRAW. By experimenting and practicing with this feature, you can take your design skills to the next level and create polished, professional graphics.

Exploring Trim Option in CorelDRAW

The Trim option in CorelDRAW is an essential feature for creating precise and polished designs. It allows users to remove overlapping or intersecting areas of objects, ensuring clean and seamless results in the final design.

How to Use the Trim Option

1. **Select the Objects**: Identify the shapes, lines, or text that require trimming and select them.
2. **Access the Trim Tool**:
    - Go to the **Arrange** menu, navigate to **Shaping**, and choose the **Trim** option.
    - Alternatively, use the shortcut key **Ctrl + Shift + F9** or right-click the selected objects and select "Trim" from the context menu.
3. **Apply the Trim**: The Trim tool will remove the intersecting areas of the selected objects, leaving the non-overlapping portions intact.

Key Benefits of the Trim Option

- **Precision**: Trim ensures that intersecting sections are removed cleanly, resulting in professional and accurate designs.
- **Versatility**: It can be used to merge shapes, remove unwanted parts, or create custom outlines and cutouts, making it an indispensable tool for complex projects.
- **Enhanced Creativity**: The Trim tool can be combined with other shaping tools like Weld, Intersect, and Combine to produce intricate and creative designs.

Tips for Using the Trim Tool

- **Experiment with Combinations**: Use Trim alongside other shaping tools to explore new possibilities and create unique designs.
- **Practice Layering**: Layer objects strategically before trimming to achieve specific effects or shapes.
- **Undo if Needed**: If the outcome isn't as expected, use the undo option (Ctrl + Z) to try different configurations.

The Trim option is a powerful tool for achieving clean and precise results in CorelDRAW projects. By mastering this feature and combining it with other tools, you can create designs that stand out with clarity and sophistication.

Mastering Intersect Option in CorelDRAW

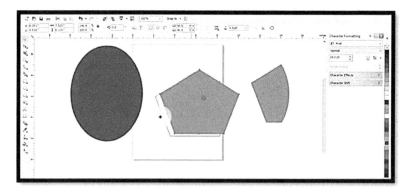

The Intersect option in CorelDRAW is a versatile feature that allows users to create complex and unique shapes by combining two or more objects. This tool is perfect for achieving intricate designs, cut-outs, and masks that might be challenging to create with other tools.

What the Intersect Option Does

The Intersect tool works by isolating the overlapping areas of selected objects and generating a new shape based on those intersecting portions. It's ideal for crafting organic shapes, custom designs, and layered effects.

Steps to Use the Intersect Option

1. **Select Objects**: Choose the objects you want to intersect. To select multiple objects, hold down the **Shift** key and click on each object.
2. **Access the Intersect Tool**:
   o Navigate to the **Shape** menu and select **Intersect** from the drop-down menu.
   o Alternatively, right-click on the selected objects and choose **Intersect** from the context menu.
3. **Create the New Shape**: After selecting the Intersect option, a new shape will be generated based on the overlapping areas, while the non-overlapping portions are removed.

Key Features and Benefits

- **Works with Colors and Fills**: The Intersect option supports objects with different fill and outline colors, enabling the creation of visually dynamic designs. You can also use varying opacity levels to add depth to your artwork.
- **Shape Modification**: In addition to creating new shapes, the Intersect tool is great for modifying existing shapes by adding cut-outs or cut-throughs, enhancing design complexity and detail.
- **Non-Destructive Editing**: The Intersect tool does not delete or alter the original objects. You can always return to the original shapes to make adjustments or refine the intersected design.

Tips for Effective Use

- **Experiment with Layers**: Try intersecting objects at different layering positions to explore creative effects.
- **Combine with Other Tools**: Use the Intersect option alongside tools like Weld, Trim, and Combine to craft truly intricate and one-of-a-kind designs.
- **Test with Gradients and Transparency**: Apply gradients or transparency to objects before intersecting them for unique shading and blending effects.

The Intersect option is a powerful way to push the boundaries of your creativity in CorelDRAW. By mastering this feature, you can design highly detailed and distinctive artwork, whether you're creating complex patterns, layered compositions, or custom shapes. Experiment with this tool to enhance your designs and discover new possibilities.

Unlocking the Power of Combine Option in CorelDRAW

The Combine option in CorelDRAW is a versatile tool that allows users to create intricate and unique designs by merging multiple objects. It opens up endless creative possibilities by enabling designers to merge, subtract, intersect, or divide shapes and paths in various ways.

Key Features of the Combine Option

1. **Merging Objects**: Combine allows you to merge two or more objects into a single shape. The resulting shape inherits the properties of the original objects, making it ideal for creating custom shapes that aren't available in the default shape tools.
2. **Subtraction**: The Combine tool can also subtract one shape from another. This feature is useful for introducing negative spaces or cut-outs, adding depth and dimension to your artwork.
3. **Intersection**: With Combine, you can create new shapes based on the overlapping areas of multiple objects. This is particularly effective for crafting intricate designs that require precise geometry or specific cut-outs.
4. **Trimming**: Combine also supports trimming, which removes the overlapping parts of objects and ensures clean, seamless intersections. This feature is essential for creating polished designs with minimal effort.

How to Use the Combine Option

1. **Select Objects**: Choose the objects you want to combine or modify.
2. **Access the Combine Tool**: Navigate to the **Arrange** menu and select **Combine**, or use the shortcut key **Ctrl + L**.
3. **Apply Modifications**: Depending on the overlapping areas and arrangement of the objects, the Combine tool will merge, subtract, or intersect shapes as required.

Benefits of Using the Combine Option

- **Custom Shapes**: Quickly create unique and complex shapes that can't be achieved with standard tools.
- **Enhanced Depth**: Add dimension to your designs with cut-outs and negative spaces.
- **Clean Intersections**: Ensure smooth and precise overlaps by trimming or merging objects seamlessly.
- **Flexibility**: Combine works well with objects of varying fill colors, outlines, and opacities, enabling diverse design possibilities.

Tips for Maximizing the Combine Tool

- **Experiment with Layers**: Position shapes strategically on different layers to explore different effects.
- **Combine with Other Tools**: Pair the Combine option with tools like Weld, Trim, and Intersect for even more complex and creative designs.
- **Use for Logos and Illustrations**: The Combine tool is particularly effective for creating intricate logos, illustrations, and artistic compositions.

By mastering the Combine option in CorelDRAW, you can unlock a new level of design potential. Whether you're crafting logos, illustrations, or intricate patterns, this tool allows you to produce unique and captivating artwork. Don't hesitate to explore its capabilities and experiment with different object combinations to make your designs stand out.

Tips and Tricks for Using Weld, Trim, Intersect, and Combine Options in CorelDRAW

Weld

- **Function**: Merges multiple shapes into a single unified object.
- **Steps**:
    1. Select the shapes you want to merge.
    2. Go to the **Shape** menu.
    3. Click **Weld**.
- **Best For**: Creating intricate or custom shapes by fusing objects or letters together.

Trim

- **Function**: Removes overlapping parts of selected shapes.
- **Steps**:
    1. Highlight the shapes to trim.
    2. Navigate to the **Shape** menu.
    3. Select **Trim**.
- **Best For**: Cutting out unnecessary portions or creating clean, sharp edges in your design.

Intersect

- **Function**: Generates a new shape from the overlapping area of selected objects.
- **Steps**:
    1. Select the objects that intersect.
    2. Go to the **Shape** menu.
    3. Click **Intersect**.
- **Best For**: Designing patterns or complex shapes that depend on shared geometry between objects.

Combine

- **Function**: Integrates shapes into a single object without removing overlapping portions.
- **Steps**:
    1. Choose the objects you want to combine.
    2. Open the **Shape** menu.
    3. Select **Combine**.
- **Best For**: Maintaining individual details within a merged object for layered or intricate designs.

Pro Tips

- **Ungroup Before Use**: Ungroup shapes for better control before applying these tools.

- **Adjust Selection Order**: Changing the order of selection can yield different results.
- **Break Apart When Needed**: Use **Break Apart** to separate combined shapes into their original forms.
- **Shortcuts**:
    - **Ctrl + Shift + X**: Trim
    - **Ctrl + Shift + L**: Intersect
    - **Ctrl + – (hyphen)**: Weld
    - **Ctrl + L**: Combine

Creative Suggestions

- Experiment with combinations of these tools to create more complex and visually engaging designs.
- Use them for a variety of projects, such as logos, patterns, and illustrations, to add depth and uniqueness to your artwork.

By using these tools effectively, you can simplify workflows, save time, and create professional-quality designs that stand out.

Grouping and Ungrouping Objects

Grouping objects is akin to affixing individual design elements together with an invisible thread, allowing for their collective movement, resizing, or transformation. When objects are grouped, they maintain their distinct properties but function as a singular entity during manipulation. This function is especially beneficial when you have a collection of elements, including text, shapes, and images, that must remain in alignment with one another to form a cohesive design. To group objects, it is necessary to initially select the elements that you wish to group. The **Pick Tool** can be employed to accomplish this. Hold down the **Shift** key and click on each object, or drag a selection box around the items you wish to include. After selecting the objects, you can combine them by selecting **Group > Group Objects** from the Object menu or by using the shortcut **Ctrl+G**. This establishes a group in which all of the specified items are considered a single object.

Benefits of Grouping

There are numerous practical advantages to grouping. Initially, it streamlines the process of aligning and relocating numerous objects. For instance, grouping guarantees that the components of a logo, which includes text, a symbol, and a background element, are appropriately aligned as they are positioned on the canvas. It is also simpler to resize multiple objects simultaneously without distorting their relationships when they are grouped. For example, the time and effort required to modify each shape will be saved by scaling a group of aligned shapes, which will preserve their alignment and proportions. An additional benefit is the uniform application of formatting, effects, or transformations. By grouping objects, it is possible to rotate them, apply shadows, or modify their colors in a single operation, thereby guaranteeing uniformity among all components.

Ungrouping Objects

The reverse procedure of ungrouping objects enables the editing or manipulation of individual elements within a group. This is especially beneficial when it is necessary to make precise modifications to a single component of a grouped design. To ungroup objects, use the **Pick Tool** to select the aggregated item and navigate to **Object > Group > Ungroup Objects**, or use the shortcut **Ctrl+U**. The individual elements can be edited independently once they have been ungrouped. It is crucial to emphasize that the properties and alignment of the individual objects are not impacted by ungrouping; rather, it eliminates the "invisible thread" that connects them. For instance, the shapes will remain in their original positions unless they are relocated if you ungroup a sequence of shapes that form a pattern.

Nested Groups

Nested groups—groups within groups—can be encountered in more intricate designs. For instance, if you generate a logo that comprises numerous layers of group elements, such as text that is grouped separately from shapes, and subsequently consolidate these elements into a single, larger group, you have established a nested group. To modify an element within a nested group, you have two options: either ungroup the entire group or utilize CorelDRAW's **Ctrl-click** functionality, which enables you to select and modify individual objects within a group without the need to ungroup.

Practical Applications of Grouping and Ungrouping

In design projects where the alignment and relationship of elements are essential, grouping is invaluable. For example, the text, logo, and decorative elements are maintained in a precise alignment when the layout of a business card is resized or repositioned by grouping them. In the same way, the organization of headings and footers across multiple pages guarantees uniformity. In contrast, ungrouping is frequently employed to refine or modify specific components of a grouped design. For instance, if you are developing a brochure and wish to modify the color of a particular section of grouped text, ungrouping enables you to isolate and modify that section without impacting the remainder of the design.

Temporary Grouping with Combine Commands

Additionally, CorelDRAW offers the capacity to temporarily manipulate grouped objects. For example, the **Combine** command can merge objects into a single shape while retaining their unique characteristics. In contrast to grouping, combining generates a new path that functions as a singular object but can be separated at a later time using the **Break Apart** command. This is especially advantageous when developing designs that require precise alignment and overlapping elements.

Aligning and Distributing Objects

Alignment is the process of arranging objects with one another or to a specific point, such as a page or a guideline. CorelDRAW offers a variety of methods for object alignment, enabling the effortless creation of symmetrical and structured designs.

When aligning objects, you have the option of aligning them relative to:
1. **The Page:** Aligns objects with the page's center, boundaries, or specific points.
2. **Other Objects:** Aligns objects with another selected object.
3. **Guidelines or Grids:** Objects are aligned according to predefined grids or manually inserted guidelines.

Use the **Pick Tool** to select the elements you wish to coordinate to align objects. Then, select **Object > Align and Distribute** or utilize the **Property Bar** to view alignment options when multiple objects are selected. The alignment options can also be accessed quickly by using shortcuts such as Ctrl+L.

CorelDRAW offers a variety of alignment options:
- **Align Left**: Aligns the left edges of selected objects.
- **Align Center**: Centers objects horizontally.
- **Align Right**: Aligns the right edges.
- **Align Top**: Align the top edges.
- **Align Middle**: Centers objects vertically.
- **Align Bottom**: Aligns the bottom edges.

Practical Use Cases for Alignment

Alignment is especially beneficial in layouts that prioritize spacing and symmetry. For example, a clean and professional appearance is guaranteed by aligning text and logo elements when designing a business card. In the same way, the alignment of headers, footers, and margins across multiple pages ensures consistency.

Distributing Objects

The act of distribution entails the uniform dispersal of numerous objects within a designated area. This is crucial when dealing with repetitive elements, such as icons, buttons, or sections of text, to establish a balanced layout. First, select all the elements that you wish to organize to distribute them. Select the appropriate distribution option by navigating to **Object > Align and Distribute**:
- **Distribute Horizontally:** Ensures that objects are equitably distributed across the horizontal axis, thereby ensuring that they are spaced uniformly.
- **Distribute Vertically:** Distribute objects with equal spacing along the vertical axis.
- **Distribute Centers:** Ensures that the center points of objects are evenly in alignment.
- **Distribute Edges:** Guarantees that the edges of objects are evenly spaced.

Additionally, CorelDRAW offers the ability to distribute objects with a reference point, such as the first object selected, a guideline, or the page itself. This is advantageous for the development of grids, rows, or columns that exhibit precise spacing.

Using the Align and Distribute Docker

The Align and Distribute Docker is available in CorelDRAW 2025 for enhanced alignment and distribution control. It can be accessed by navigating to **Window > Dockers > Align and Distribute**. **This panel offers sophisticated alternatives, including:**
- Aligning objects with a particular key object.
- Conforming to a custom guideline, margin, or page.
- Determining the precise spacing between distributed objects.

As an illustration, the docker can be employed to guarantee that each icon is evenly spaced and aligned with the top of the menu bar when organizing icons.

Practical Applications of Distribution

In designs that necessitate consistent spacing of multiple elements, distribution is essential. For instance,
- A balanced layout can be achieved by equitably distributing text sections in a flyer.
- Distributing objects assures uniform spacing, thereby improving the visual appeal, when creating a grid of product images for an e-commerce website.
- The uniform distribution of iconography or data elements in infographics is beneficial for preserving readability and clarity.

Combining Alignment and Distribution

Alignment and distribution are frequently employed in conjunction to enhance precision. For example, in the context of a poster design, it may be beneficial to position a subheading and heading in the center of the page, while bullet points are distributed uniformly below. This assures a refined and cohesive layout by combining these functions.

Tips for Effective Alignment and Distribution

1. **Use Grids and Guidelines:** To facilitate manual alignment, activate grids and rulers from the **View** menu. Custom reference points can be established by dragging guidelines from the rulers.
2. **Snap Features:** Utilize the **Snap To** option in the **View** menu to enable the precise alignment and distribution of elements by attaching them to objects, grids, or guidelines.
3. **Grouping:** Before aligning or distributing, organize elements that are related to guarantee that they remain in their designated locations. For instance, organize a logo and its corresponding text to ensure that they function as a cohesive unit.
4. **Custom Spacing:** Utilize the **Align and Distribute Docker** to establish precise distances between objects during distribution.

CHAPTER FOUR
VECTOR GRAPHICS ESSENTIALS
What Are Vector Graphics?

Vector graphics are a form of computer graphics that employ mathematical equations to define points, curves, lines, and shapes. Vector graphics, in contrast to raster graphics, are generated through the use of paths that are both resolution-independent and scalable instead of a fixed grid of pixels. Vector images are ideal for designs that necessitate precision and versatility, as they can be resized indefinitely without compromising quality. This makes them suitable for use in logos, illustrations, and typography.

How Vector Graphics Work

Paths are the fundamental components of vector graphics. A path is a line that connects two or more points, known as anchor points, with either straight or curved segments. The computer can reproduce the image at any dimension without any distortion or pixelation, as these paths are defined by mathematical formulas. For instance, a circle in vector format is defined by its mathematical curve, center point, and radius, rather than a collection of colored squares (pixels).

The attributes of each path in a vector graphic may include:
- **Stroke:** The shape's outline, which encompasses its thickness and manner.
- **Fill:** The interior color or pattern of the shape.
- **Effects:** Features such as transparency, shadows, or gradients.

The underlying structure of the graphic is not affected by the editing or adjustment of these attributes, as they are applied dynamically.

Key Features of Vector Graphics

1. **Resolution Independence:** The capacity of vector graphics to scale without sacrificing quality is one of their most noteworthy benefits. The lines and contours of a vector logo remain crisp and clear, regardless of whether it is enlarged to suit a billboard or shrunk to fit a business card.
2. **Smaller File Sizes:** Vector graphics are typically smaller in size than raster graphics, which store data for each pixel, as they only contain the mathematical equations that define paths.
3. **Editability:** Each component of a vector graphic is capable of being independently modified. Designers can modify colors, shapes, and sizes without compromising the quality of the graphic or impacting other elements.
4. **Layered Structure:** Layers are frequently employed in vector graphics to facilitate the organization of elements, thereby simplifying the management of intricate designs that contain numerous components.
5. **Device Agnostic:** Vector graphics appear identical on all devices, including printers and displays, because their resolution is not associated with a particular output.

Common Uses of Vector Graphics

1. **Logos and Branding:** Vector graphics are the industry standard for logo design due to their ability to be resized without sacrificing detail. This guarantees that logos are depicted clearly on a variety of surfaces, including billboards and websites.
2. **Illustrations:** Vector graphics are employed by artists and illustrators to generate intricate caricatures, infographics, and drawings. The capacity to manipulate paths and shapes enables the implementation of precise adjustments.
3. **Typography:** Text in vector format is optimal for digital designs and printed materials, as it remains readable and precise at any scale.
4. **Technical Drawings:** Vector graphics are employed by engineers and architects for CAD (Computer-Aided Design) illustrations, which necessitate precise measurements and scalability.
5. **Web Graphics:** Scalable Vector Graphics (SVG), a web-compatible vector format, are frequently employed for illustrations, animations, and icons on websites. It guarantees consistent quality and rapid loading times on all devices.
6. **Print Media:** Vector graphics are essential in print design because they guarantee that text, logos, and images remain distinct and legible, even at high resolutions.

Vector Graphics vs. Raster Graphics

The methods by which vector graphics are generated, stored, and utilized are substantially different from those of raster graphics.

- **Raster Graphics:** Raster graphics, composed of pixels (e.g., JPEG, PNG, BMP), are resolution-dependent. Pixelation or blurring occurs when a raster image is enlarged beyond its original resolution.
- **Vector Graphics:** Vector graphics are mathematically defined as graphics that maintain their sharpness regardless of their scale. They are particularly well-suited for designs that necessitate scaling, such as logos or print arrangements.

For instance, because the quality of a raster image of a circle is dependent on the number of pixels it contains, it may appear pixelated when enlarged. Nevertheless, a vector circle will maintain its smooth, pointed edges regardless of the extent of its resizing.

Common Vector File Formats

- **CDR:** The native format of CorelDRAW, which is optimal for saving editable vector designs.
- **AI:** The native format of Adobe Illustrator, which is extensively, employed in professional design workflows.
- **SVG:** Scalable Vector Graphics is a web-friendly format that is designed for online use.
- **EPS:** Encapsulated PostScript, a format that is frequently employed for high-quality printing.
- **PDF:** Portable Document Format, which is capable of containing vector elements for printing or sharing.

Advantages of Using Vector Graphics

1. **Scalability:** Vector graphics are suitable for projects that necessitate flexibility, such as brand assets or multi-platform campaigns, as they can be resized to any dimension without sacrificing quality.
2. **High Quality:** Vectors guarantee that lines, text, and shapes are crisp and clear, even at extremely high resolutions.
3. **Editing Efficient:** Designers can make changes rapidly without having to start from the beginning, as vector objects are simple to manipulate.
4. **Reusable Components:** Vector graphics elements can be repurposed and reused, which can reduce the time required for iterative design processes.

Disadvantages of Vector Graphics

1. **Limited Photorealism:** Vector graphics are not suitable for images that necessitate the nuance of raster graphics, such as photographs, which are highly detailed.
2. **Software Dependency:** Specialized software, such as CorelDRAW, Adobe Illustrator, or Inkscape, is frequently necessary for the creation and modification of vector graphics.
3. **Learning Curve:** For novices, the acquisition of vector graphic tools and techniques may necessitate a significant amount of time.

Software for Creating Vector Graphics

There are numerous tools available for the creation and modification of vector graphics:
- **CorelDRAW:** A favorite among designers, CorelDRAW is renowned for its intuitive interface and potent vector tools.
- **Adobe Illustrator:** A professional-grade software that offers a wide range of features for vector design.
- **Inkscape:** A free, open-source alternative that possesses comprehensive vector capabilities.

Working with Nodes and Paths

Getting Started with Node Editing

Node editing is the process of modifying shapes and paths by adding, altering, and removing nodes. CorelDRAW provides designers with the ability to manipulate curves and angles through the use of various node varieties, including cusp, smooth, and symmetrical. The **Shape Tool** allows users to modify curves and lines by dragging nodes, changing their categories, and moving control handles. Additionally, users can manipulate multiple nodes simultaneously, join various shapes, and reverse the start and end nodes to create intricate designs. It is essential to comprehend the functions and interactions of each node type to conquer the art of node editing. Designers can generate intricate, scalable vector art with precision and detail as a result of this adaptability.

Essential Node Tools in CorelDRAW

CorelDRAW provides users with the ability to precisely manipulate vector art through the use of comprehensive node editing tools. Each tool improves the creative process, from the precise selection of nodes to the comprehension of various node types.

Selecting Nodes with Precision

Accurately selecting nodes in CorelDRAW is essential for detailed modification. Central to this endeavor is the **Shape Tool**. It allows users to select multiple nodes simultaneously by clicking and dragging. Users can further refine their selections by zooming in on specific regions. Detailed and refined designs are achieved by the precise selection of nodes, which enables the manipulation of curves and lines without influencing other components of the artwork. Toggling between various selections modes is possible for advanced users through the use of shortcuts. They can rapidly refine their choices by employing straightforward key combinations. This feature is particularly beneficial when working with intricate vector images, as precision is essential.

Adding and Deleting Nodes

The process of adding and deleting nodes is both efficient and straightforward in CorelDRAW. By double-clicking on curves, users can incorporate nodes into the **Shape Tool**. In contrast, nodes can be eliminated by selecting them and clicking the delete key. This adaptability enables users to make modifications to designs without the need to start fresh, as vector paths can be adjusted effortlessly. In addition to the addition and deletion of nodes, users can join or break them as necessary. Shapes can be simplified by joining nodes, while more complex designs can be achieved by separating them. The process is made seamless and workflow is improved by CorelDRAW's intuitive interface, which facilitates these actions.

Node Types and Their Functions

User control over vector trajectories is improved by comprehending the varieties of nodes in CorelDRAW. Each of the three types of nodes—**cusp, smooth**, and **symmetrical**—has a specified purpose. Cusp nodes are advantageous for corners, as they enable the creation of acute angles. Gentle curves are generated by smooth nodes, which are optimal for fluid designs. Symmetrical nodes are crucial for maintaining the equilibrium of curves on either side, which is necessary for symmetrical elements. The process of selecting and modifying specific nodes is simplified by the **unique shapes** that are allotted to each type, which enables easy identification of these node types. The manipulation capabilities of users are enhanced by the mastery of node types, which enables them to accomplish the desired effects in their vector artwork with precision and efficiency.

Advanced Node Editing Techniques

Vector art can be precisely adjusted through the use of advanced node manipulation in CorelDRAW. This encompasses the seamless cutting and joining of paths, the manipulation of Bezier handles for curves, and the conversion of text to curves for comprehensive adjustments. Each technique enhances the creative process by providing control over design elements.

Working with Bezier Handles

Bezier handles in CorelDRAW are essential tools for precisely adjusting the contours of shapes and lines. By clicking on a node and extending its handles, users can control the angle and tension of curves, creating smooth and seamless transitions between connected paths.

Key Features of Bezier Handles

1. **Precise Adjustments**: Handles allow designers to fine-tune curves, making them smoother or sharper as needed.
2. **Visual Feedback**: CorelDRAW highlights node types—such as apex, smooth, or symmetrical—which helps users understand how each node affects the curve and provides better control over paths.

Node Types and Their Functions

- **Apex Nodes**: Used for sharp angles or corners in a design.
- **Smooth Nodes**: Create gradual transitions between connected paths.
- **Symmetrical Nodes**: Ensure uniform tension on both sides of the curve, resulting in balanced arcs.

Benefits of Mastering Bezier Handles

- **Fluid Designs**: Proper adjustment of Bezier handles ensures that design elements flow naturally, an essential aspect of professional vector artwork.
- **Creative Control**: Understanding and manipulating nodes and handles gives designers the freedom to create intricate shapes and graceful curves.
- **Polished Results**: Mastering these techniques allows for the creation of seamless and visually appealing designs.

Tips for Effective Use

- **Practice Regularly**: Becoming proficient with Bezier handles takes time, but regular practice will improve your ability to craft smooth and complex shapes.
- **Experiment with Nodes**: Test different node types to see how they affect your curves and adjust accordingly.
- **Use Zoom for Precision**: When working on detailed sections, zoom in to make more accurate adjustments to nodes and handles.

Mastering Bezier handles not only enhances your design precision but also elevates the quality of your vector art, enabling you to create flowing, professional-grade graphics with ease.

Cutting and Joining Paths

CorelDRAW allows designers to modify shapes and create new forms by cutting and joining paths, providing flexibility for custom designs.

Cutting Paths

- **Tool Used**: The **Shape Tool** is essential for splitting paths.
- **How It Works**: Select the **Shape Tool**, click on any part of the path, and divide it into two separate sections.
- **Use Case**: Perfect for dividing shapes or paths into distinct parts, allowing for more detailed editing and customization.

Joining Paths

- **Process**:
    1. Select the nodes at the endpoints of each path.
    2. Use the **Join** option to connect the paths.
- **Outcome**: This method merges two paths into a single continuous form, enabling the creation of complex designs from simpler components.

These techniques are invaluable for customizing designs without starting from scratch. By cutting and joining paths, designers can experiment with shapes and forms, fostering creativity and adaptability.

Converting Text to Curves for Editing

CorelDRAW allows text to be converted into editable vector outlines, enabling designers to reshape and customize typography.

How to Convert Text to Curves

1. Select the text you want to modify.
2. Use the **Convert to Curves** command (shortcut: **Ctrl + Q**).
3. Each character is transformed into an individual shape.

Advantages

- **Custom Typography**: After conversion, each letter can be reshaped and stylized, making it ideal for logos or special effects.
- **Creative Freedom**: Designers gain complete control over the letterforms, enabling unique designs beyond the constraints of standard fonts.

Considerations

- Once converted, the text is no longer editable as traditional text.
- This process is best used for projects requiring full artistic customization, such as branding and bespoke typography.

Refining Shapes and Paths

Refinement in CorelDRAW involves enhancing the quality of vector art by applying creative effects to nodes, aligning paths, and improving contours.

Smoothing Paths

- **Purpose**: Converts jagged or angular lines into smooth, flowing curves.
- **How to Use**:
    1. Select the path with the **Shape Tool**.
    2. Drag nodes manually for fine-tuning or apply the **Smooth Node** option for automatic refinement.
- **Result**: Sleek and professional-looking curves.

Straightening Paths

- **Purpose**: Adjusts uneven or irregular lines into precise, linear shapes.
- **How to Use**:
    1. Select specific nodes using the **Shape Tool**.
    2. Use the straightening feature to create clean lines.
- **Result**: Crisp and precise linear elements, ideal for structured designs.

By combining smoothing and straightening techniques, designers can achieve refined artwork that balances fluidity and precision.

Tips for Enhanced Path Manipulation

1. **Node Management**: Regularly align and adjust nodes to ensure smooth transitions and clean shapes.
2. **Experiment**: Use cutting and joining paths to test new forms without committing to permanent changes.
3. **Maintain Flexibility**: Keep original shapes in a separate layer to allow for revisions if needed.

Mastering these techniques in CorelDRAW empowers designers to create polished, professional, and highly customized artwork while maintaining flexibility and precision.

Aligning and Distributing Nodes

Proper alignment and distribution of nodes are fundamental for maintaining balance and consistency in designs.

Alignment

- Nodes can be aligned to axes or edges by selecting multiple nodes and using alignment tools.
- This ensures that components are positioned precisely, contributing to a polished and cohesive design.

Distribution

- Distribution tools enable nodes to be evenly spaced along a path.
- Adjusting the proximity of nodes ensures uniformity, especially useful for creating grids or patterns where consistency is critical.

By using these tools, designers can exercise greater control over their artwork's structure, resulting in well-balanced and professional designs.

Contouring and Blending for Visual Effects

Contouring

- **Definition**: Adds layers around a shape to create depth and interest.
- **How It Works**: Select the object, and then adjust the contour depth and the number of layers.
- **Use Case**: Ideal for adding complexity and richness to designs by building layers of visual elements.

Blending

- **Definition**: Combines multiple shapes into a single smooth gradient, merging their paths seamlessly.
- **How It Works**: Select the shapes and use the Blend Tool to create a transition between them.
- **Use Case**: Frequently used for dynamic transitions and effects in vector art, enhancing movement and flow in the design.

Mastering these tools allows designers to elevate their artwork, adding professional-quality details and engaging visual elements.

Efficiency Tips for Node Editing in CorelDRAW

Improving efficiency while working with nodes can significantly streamline the design process. Here are some strategies:

1. **Repetition for Uniformity**: Apply repeatable techniques to maintain consistency across designs.
2. **Custom Toolbars**: Configure toolbars to provide quick access to frequently used tools.
3. **Utilize Shortcuts**: Memorize shortcuts for common tasks to save time and minimize disruptions.

Using Shortcuts for a Faster Workflow

Shortcuts play a crucial role in optimizing workflow when editing nodes in CorelDRAW:

- **Selecting Nodes**:
  - Use the **Ctrl** key to quickly select multiple nodes without individually clicking on each one.
  - The **Shift** key allows you to add or remove nodes from a selection with ease.

- **Quick Corrections**:
  - ○ **Ctrl + Z**: Undo the last action.
  - ○ **Ctrl + Y**: Redo the last action.
- **General Efficiency**:
  - ○ Keep one hand on the mouse and the other on the keyboard to maintain workflow momentum.
  - ○ Memorize frequently used shortcuts to reduce time spent navigating menus.

Customizing Toolbars for Node Editing

CorelDRAW enables users to tailor their workspace by customizing toolbars to suit their specific needs.

How to Customize Toolbars

1. Navigate to the **Toolbar Settings** in the interface.
2. Drag and drop frequently used tools, such as the Shape Tool or Point Reduction Tool, into a new or existing toolbar.
3. Adjust the size and position of the toolbar to fit your workflow preferences.

Benefits

- Critical tools are always accessible; reducing the time spent navigating menus.
- Personalized toolbars enhance productivity by aligning the interface with individual design habits.
- Customization adds a personal touch that improves the overall vector design experience.

Repeating and Cloning for Design Consistency

CorelDRAW offers powerful cloning and repetition features to help maintain uniformity in designs while minimizing manual effort.

Features

- **Copy and Paste**: Quickly duplicate elements with standard shortcuts.
- **Ctrl + D Shortcut**: Instantly replicate selected objects, creating consistent patterns or symmetrical layouts.

Use Cases

- **Patterns**: Develop recurring elements, such as grids or decorative motifs, with precise alignment.
- **Symmetry**: Ensure uniformity across all parts of a design by cloning nodes or paths for technical drawings or logos.

This approach is a time-saver for projects that demand accuracy and consistency while minimizing manual adjustments.

Practical Applications of Node Editing

Node editing in CorelDRAW plays a vital role in improving the quality of vector artwork across various projects. Here are two examples of real-world applications:

1. Creating Logos with Precision

- **Importance of Precision**: Logos must look professional and consistent at all sizes.
- **Node Editing Tools**:
    - Use the **Shape Tool** to refine curves and lines.
    - Add or remove nodes as needed to enhance clarity and balance.
    - Assign node types (e.g., cusp or smooth) to achieve sharp angles or fluid curves.
- **Outcome**: A polished, high-quality logo that reflects attention to detail and craftsmanship.

2. Designing Custom Typography

- **Why It Matters**: Custom typography adds a distinctive character to projects, making them unique and memorable.
- **Techniques**:
    - Use node manipulation to adjust the shape of each letter.
    - Marquee-select multiple nodes to edit several elements simultaneously.
    - Align and space characters consistently to maintain a cohesive look.
- **Outcome**: Unique, professional typography tailored to the project's needs.

Working with Paths

One of the fundamental components of the creation and modification of vector graphics in CorelDRAW 2025 is the use of paths. The backbone of every vector object is a path, which is essentially a line or curve defined by anchor points and segments. By mastering paths, it is possible to manipulate objects with precision, refine designs, and create intricate shapes. It is imperative to comprehend the concept of paths to fully realize the potential of vector graphics, regardless of whether you are creating intricate illustrations or drawing a straightforward line.

What Are Paths?

Vector graphics are composed of paths. They are composed of:

1. **Anchor Points:** These are the points that define a path. Anchor points can be either smooth points (which create arcs) or corner points (which create acute angles).
2. **Segment:** Anchor points are connected by lines or curves known as segments. The manipulation of segments can result in either a linear or curved shape.
3. **Control Handles:** These are located on smooth anchor points and enable the user to modify the curvature of the segments.

Paths may be either **open** (a straight or curved line with distinct start and end locations) or **closed** (a continuous path that is shaped like a circle or polygon).

Creating Paths

For path creation, CorelDRAW offers a variety of tools, each of which is tailored to the specific requirements of the design:

1. **Freehand Tool:**

- o The Freehand Tool enables the user to draw paths effortlessly, emulating a natural drawing motion. To generate a curve or line, merely click and drag.
- o To achieve smoother lines, modify the smoothing settings in the **Property Bar** to reduce the number of anchor points.

2. **Bezier Tool:**
   - o The Bezier Tool is the optimal choice for the creation of precise paths. It enables the manual placement of anchor points and the adjustment of control handles to determine the curvature of each segment.
   - o Place a linear segment by clicking, or construct a curve by clicking and dragging.

3. **Pen Tool:**
   - o The Pen Tool is a more intuitive alternative to the Bezier Tool, allowing you to construct paths by clicking on corner points or by clicking and dragging to create curved segments. Drawing intricate shapes is a prevalent preference.

4. **Shape Tools:**
   - o Custom paths can be initiated by utilizing basic shapes such as rectangles, ellipses, and polygons. Convert these shapes to curves (**Ctrl+Q**) to modify their trajectories after they have been generated.

Editing Paths

Path editing is the process by which you can enhance and perfect your designs. CorelDRAW provides a diverse array of tools and methods for path adjustment:

1. **Shape Tool (F10):**
   - • The Shape Tool is the principal tool for editing trajectories. Please select a path and utilize this tool to:
   - o **Move Anchor Points:** To modify the path's geometry, drag anchor points.
   - o **Add or Remove Anchor Points:** To simplify or improve the path, right-click on a segment and add or remove points.
   - o **Adjust Control Handles:** To refine curves, drag the handles on flat points.
   - • To modify the type of node (e.g., corner, smooth, or symmetrical), utilize the **Property Bar**.

2. **Convert to curves:**
   - o To enable the editing of fundamental shapes, select the object and navigate to **Object > Convert to Curves** or press **Ctrl+Q**. This converts the object into a path that can be manipulated.

3. **Breaking and Joining Paths:**
   - o Divide a path into distinct segments by employing the **Break Apart** command. Right-click on the path and select **Break Apart**.
   - o To connect two open trajectories, ensure that their endpoints overlap, then select them and utilize the **Join Curves** option in the Property Bar.

4. **Smoothing Paths:**
   - o Use the Smooth Tool to reduce the number of anchor points and create clearer lines for uneven or irregular paths. Increased control is achieved by adjusting the tool's intensity in the Property Bar.

5. **Stretch and Transform:**

o The **Pick Tool** enables the stretching, scaling, rotation, and skewing of paths. Use the transformation options in the **Property Bar** or select the path and drag the handles.

Advanced Path Techniques

1. **Blending Paths:** The Blend Tool generates a sequence of intermediate shapes that serve as a seamless transition between two paths. For example, the combination of two curved paths can result in the creation of dynamic, fluid designs.
2. **PowerClip with Paths:** Employ the **PowerClip** feature to insert images or objects within a path. This is especially beneficial for the creation of custom shapes or coverings that are filled with textures or photographs.
3. **Path Effects:** CorelDRAW offers a variety of path effects, such as:
   - **Contour:** Incorporates concentric shapes within or outside of a path.
   - **Envelope:** Transforms trajectories by managing their encompassing box.
   - **Extrude:** A 3D effect is generated by incorporating depth into a path.
4. **Converting Text to Paths:** Paths can be generated from text to facilitate precise customization. To convert the text to curves, select it and then press **Ctrl+Q**. This enables the editing of individual letters as paths, which is ideal for the development of personalized typography.

Aligning and Snapping Paths

CorelDRAW provides tools to guarantee precision when working with paths:
- **Snapping:** Facilitate the effortless alignment of paths by enabling snapping to grids, guidelines, or other objects.
- **Align and Distribute Docker:** Utilize this function to align paths with the canvas or other elements.

Exporting and Using Paths

Paths generated in CorelDRAW can be exported to a variety of formats for integration with other applications.
- **SVG:** Suitable for scalable designs and web use.
- **AI/EPS:** For professional printing workflows and compatibility with Adobe Illustrator.
- **DXF/DWG:** For technical drawings in CAD applications.

Common Challenges and Tips

1. **Avoid Excessive Anchor Points:** An excessive number of anchor points can exacerbate the difficulty of editing paths and increase the size of the file. Utilize refining tools or simplify paths whenever feasible.
2. **Maintain Proportions:** When scaling paths, hold **Shift** to conserve proportions and avoid distortion.
3. **Experiment with Path Effects:** Path effects can lend visual interest to your designs. Do not hesitate to experiment with contours, distortions, and composites.

Using the Pen Tool

The Pen Tool in CorelDRAW is indispensable for the development of precise vector art. It is an invaluable tool for detailed projects, as it enables users to generate seamless curves and straight lines. Discover the functionality of this utility and its location within CorelDRAW by reading the following.

Pen Tool Overview

For any digital artist employing CorelDRAW, the Pen Tool is indispensable. It enables users to create both straight and curved lines with exceptional precision. Shapes can be created by connecting each line, or "path." This is essential for the production of scalable, clean vector images that maintain quality at any scale. Designers can achieve the desired aesthetic by modifying the nodes on these paths, which allows them to alter the curves and angles. This control facilitates the replication of complex imagery or the creation of intricate designs. An artist's workflow can be considerably improved by comprehending this functionality, which enables more efficient and effective design processes.

Accessing the Pen Tool in CorelDRAW

The Pen Tool is easily accessible in CorelDRAW. First, locate the toolbar on the left-hand side of the interface. Locate an icon that resembles a fountain pen nib. The Pen Tool is symbolized by this icon. To activate the pen icon, users may either select it or enter the **P** key on their keyboard. They can then commence the process of establishing channels. Anchor points are established by clicking on the canvas, which is connected by paths. The anchor points can be clicked and dragged to transition between straight and curved trajectories. This attribute enables the Pen Tool to serve as an adaptable asset in any digital design endeavor.

Mastering Pen Tool Basics

Mastering CorelDRAW's Pen Tool necessitates a combination of fundamental shape comprehension, straight line creation, and curved path navigation. Users can acquire the necessary skills to create professional-quality vector art by concentrating on these components.

Starting with Simple Shapes

The Pen Tool is an excellent starting point for generating basic shapes. Users may commence their practice by employing fundamental shapes, such as circles, squares, or triangles. This can be accomplished in CorelDRAW by selecting to establish anchor points, which will connect each point to form the desired shape.

Tips

- Utilize the grid and snap-to-grid functions to guarantee precision.

- Conduct experiments with the stroke and fill options to observe the immediate transformations that occur as shapes are formed.

Once you are at ease, progress to slightly more intricate shapes by incorporating additional anchor points and adjusting their positioning. This practice will facilitate the development of the fundamental skills necessary for the creation of more intricate artwork.

Creating Straight Lines

Vector art is predicated on the use of straight lines. They are the foundation of numerous designs. By selecting to establish anchor points, users can generate straight lines with CorelDRAW's Pen Tool. Each stroke establishes a straight line between two locations.

Steps:
1. Choose the **Pen Tool**.
2. To establish the first anchor point, simply click.
3. The second anchor point must be clicked again to establish a line between them.

Continue to incorporate anchor points to generate intricate shapes. It is imperative to close paths by selecting the initial point to create closed shapes. Employ the rulers and guides to ensure that the line lengths and angles are consistent and aligned.

Drawing Curved Paths

Vector art is enhanced by the incorporation of curved paths, which foster dynamism and fluidity. Anchor points are established and control handles are employed to form contours with the Pen Tool.

Process:
- Utilize a click to establish the initial anchor point.
- To modify the trajectory, click and drag the second anchor point.
- The curve can be adjusted by repositioning the handles to increase or decrease its prominence.

To achieve mastery, it is necessary to comprehend the effective use of control handles. The curve's angle and length are modified by adjusting these handles, which provides precise control over the path. Iterative practice is essential for the development of these abilities and the creation of sophisticated, curved vector graphics.

Advanced Pen Tool Techniques

The quality of your vector art can be improved by mastering CorelDRAW's Pen Tool. In this section, we examine essential techniques, including the addition and deletion of anchor points, the modification of Bezier handles, and the conversion of anchors from corner to smooth.

Adding and Deleting Anchor Points

The precise control of vector paths is facilitated by the addition and deletion of anchor points. Artists can generate more intricate and detailed curves by incorporating anchor points. Keeping the path clear and straightforward is facilitated by eliminating superfluous anchor points. This also reduces the file size in addition to simplifying shapes. The **Shape Tool** is frequently employed in CorelDRAW to add points by selecting the path where the new point should be set. Users may eliminate an anchor point by selecting it and pressing the eliminate key. It is crucial to guarantee that the adjustment following the deletion is seamless to preserve the uniformity of the curved lines.

Adjusting Bezier Handles

Bezier handles are essential for the formation of curves. Users can modify the direction and steepness of the curves by extending or retracting these controls. This is imperative for obtaining the desirable shapes and smooth transitions. Users can view the handles by clicking on an anchor point in CorelDRAW. The symmetry of the handles can be disrupted by holding down the **Alt** key (on Windows) or the **Option** key (on Mac), which provides individual control over each side. The ability to independently adjust these handles allows for the fine adjustment of each curve segment to align with the specific design requirements.

Converting Anchors from Corner to Smooth

The behavior of trajectories is altered by converting anchors between corner and smooth points. Paths undergo abrupt changes in direction at corner locations. Gentle contours are generated by smooth points. In CorelDRAW, paths with flat points flow more organically, rendering them suitable for organic shapes such as circles or waves. By selecting the anchor and employing the "**Convert to Curve**" option, users can convert corner points to smooth. The vector art's overall flow and aesthetic are enhanced by the seamless integration of both sharp and fluid lines in a single design, which is facilitated by this flexibility in transitioning.

Creating Complex Vector Shapes

CorelDRAW's Pen Tool can transform basic designs into intricate compositions by enabling the creation of complex vector shapes. To produce detailed and precise vector artwork, it is imperative to employ critical techniques such as layer management, path combining, and path intersection management.

Combining Multiple Paths

The ability to combine multiple paths in CorelDRAW enables the construction of complex shapes from fundamental components. Users may initiate the process by utilizing the Pen Tool to create distinct paths. The **combined** command can be employed to merge these trajectories after they have been drawn. This command assists in the formation of a continuous path from a series of lesser paths, while simultaneously preserving the distinctive characteristics of each path. The **Weld** and **Trim** functions can also be employed by designers to streamline trajectories. These tools are especially beneficial for the development of personalized designs that necessitate a combination of straight lines and curves. Diverse vector designs can be achieved by experimenting with various combinations, thereby maximizing the Pen Tool's adaptability.

Utilizing Layers for Complex Artwork

In CorelDRAW, layers are a potent tool for organizing and managing intricate artwork. Artists can achieve a higher degree of control and flexibility by separating distinct components of their designs using layers.

For example, strata can be designated for the placement of detailed components. This division is advantageous when it comes to modifying specific regions of the artwork without affecting other components. Additionally, layers simplify the process of revising and adjusting. By hiding, locking, or arranging layers, designers can concentrate on specific elements, thereby increasing the efficiency of the creative process. In projects with a high number of components, the incorporation of descriptive names into layers facilitates navigation and organization.

Working with Path Intersection

Path intersection is a method that increases the intricacy of vector structures. This necessitates the utilization of tools such as the **Intersect** command in CorelDRAW. This command enables the intersection of two or more overlapping trajectories to generate a new shape. It is a convenient feature for creating intricate patterns or detailed components of an artwork. Artists can generate distinctive shapes by experimenting with interlocking paths and modifying nodes. Stunning visual effects can be achieved when two paths intersect at precisely selected points, and this approach fosters creativity.

Efficiency Tips and Tricks

The CorelDRAW Pen Tool has the potential to significantly improve productivity and accuracy by enhancing efficiency. Key strategies involve the effective use of snap-to features and keyboard shortcuts.

Using Shortcuts for the Pen Tool

The design process can be significantly expedited by utilizing keyboard shortcuts. Designers can rapidly transition between tools by memorizing and employing specific shortcuts. Essential shortcuts in CorelDRAW include **F5** for selecting the Pen Tool and **Ctrl+Z** for rectifying errors. Pressing the **Spacebar** is another useful shortcut for transitioning between the Pen Tool and the most recently used tool. This toggling enables the seamless transition of design duties. Learning these alternatives can result in a more uninterrupted creative flow by reducing the time spent browsing through menus. It can be advantageous for individuals who are still in the process of learning or who occasionally neglect shortcuts to keep a reference sheet readily available. The utilization of these shortcuts to establish muscle memory results in a more efficient design process.

Leveraging Snap-To Features

Snap-to capabilities are indispensable for attaining precise alignments without the necessity for continuous manual adjustments. Designers can guarantee that nodes and lines are precisely aligned with existing shapes and guidelines by enabling features such as Snap to Objects. Maintenance of consistent spacing and alignment throughout the design is facilitated by the utilization of **Snap to Grid.** It is especially beneficial for novices who wish to maintain orderly and organized proportions. Another useful tip is the utilization of Snap to Guidelines, which aids in the precise positioning of elements along predetermined lines. This minimizes the time required to make minute adjustments and guarantees a more refined final product. The utilization of these features can enhance the precision of vector art projects in CorelDRAW and save time.

Practical Applications of the Pen Tool

The pen tool in CorelDRAW is a highly effective tool for the creation of precise vector art. It is indispensable for the development of distinctive logos, the creation of intricate illustrations, and the improvement of typography through the use of personalized calligraphy.

Designing Logos with the Pen Tool

The pen tool is an essential tool for the development of emblems. Designers employ it to create insignia that are distinctive by utilizing crisp lines and shapes. The pen tool enables the creation of logo designs that are both simple and complex by enabling the creation of seamless contours and angles. The tool provides precise control over anchor points and paths in addition to the ability to create shapes. This guarantees that each element of the logo is precisely aligned. This precision is vital in preserving the quality and clarity of the logo, even when it is necessary to resize it. Additionally, the stylus tool facilitates a more personalized approach to logo design. Designers can employ it to generate distinctive components that distinguish a brand from its competitors. This customization has the potential to imbue logos with a distinctive, memorable quality that resonates with audiences.

Crafting Detailed Illustrations

The pen tool is particularly adept at creating intricate illustrations. It is employed by artists to trace and generate intricate shapes that are challenging to produce with other tools. This ability is indispensable for the creation of intricate, high-quality artwork. Artists are capable of creating genuine images by employing precise control over lines and contours. The pen tool provides versatility, whether it is used to generate organic shapes or precise geometric patterns. This renders it indispensable for both digital illustrations and the replication of hand-drawn styles. Another benefit is the capacity to modify shapes seamlessly without sacrificing quality. This implies that modifications can be implemented at any point during the creative process. The pen tool's adaptability enables artists to perpetually refine and experiment with their illustrations.

Pen Tool for Typography and Lettering

The pen tool has also significantly improved typography. It enables designers to create unique lettering styles and typefaces that are not present in standard font libraries. Designers can manipulate letterforms with precision, guaranteeing that each character is both flawless and unique. The pen tool is a tool in the development of lettering that is both elegant and seamless in its integration with insignia and other designs. Designers can execute each curve and angle of the letters with precision by modifying anchor points. This results in text that is both professional and tidy. Additionally, the pen tool facilitates an abundance of creativity when employed for lettering. Designers can either develop new letterforms or modify existing ones to achieve the desired aesthetic. This liberation presents an infinite number of opportunities for typography that is both expressive and impactful.

Best Practices for Pen Tool Precision

Attention to detail and practice is necessary to master the Pen Tool in CorelDRAW. The quality of vector art can be considerably improved by comprehending the techniques for creating smooth curves, maintaining a consistent line weight, and managing complex adjustments.

Achieving Smooth Curves

The Pen Tool necessitates the effective utilization of anchor points to generate seamless contours. To guarantee more seamless transitions between curves, it is recommended that users implement a reduced number of anchor points. The exquisite contours are primarily determined by the position and angle of the handles. Maintaining the natural flow of the lines can be achieved by adjusting the handles symmetrically. Another beneficial suggestion is to increase the magnification level while performing these modifications. This enables more precise alignment and finer control. The artwork is visually appealing due to the balanced approach between anchor point placement and handle positioning, which results in smooth curves.

Consistency in Line Weight

A refined appearance in vector art is facilitated by the consistent use of line weight. Setting a consistent stroke weight that corresponds with the design's theme is advantageous for CorelDRAW users. The software's tools should be employed to meticulously modify the line weight throughout the artwork. It can be difficult to maintain consistent line weight, but the use of templates and guidelines can be beneficial. Users guarantee that the thickness of lines remains consistent by comparing various regions of the artwork. This meticulous attention to detail is vital in the development of a cohesive design.

Maintaining Control over Complex Edits

The Pen Tool necessitates precision and perseverance to manage intricate adjustments. The procedure is simplified by deconstructing a complex shape into smaller, more manageable segments. Users are encouraged to address each section individually to guarantee accuracy and control. Complex adjustments are effectively managed through the utilization of layers. Users can modify specific components without influencing the entire design by working on various layers. This method safeguards other components from unintentional modifications while emphasizing the intricate components of the artwork.

How to Use the Outline Pen Tool

In this section, we will explore the diverse capabilities of the Outline tools. There are numerous methods for obtaining access to the settings of these tools, such as:
- The Outline Tools tool category in the Toolbox is available for Windows only.
- Keyboard shortcuts: **F12** for Windows and **CMD + SHIFT + P** for Mac.
- The outline tab on the Properties docker (Properties Inspector for Mac).
- Outline swatch on the status bar.
- Property bar.

The toolkit that extends along the left side of the CorelDRAW interface does not display these tools by default. The Outline Tools can be added to the toolkit by Windows users by selecting the plus icon at the bottom of the toolbox, scrolling down to the end of the list, and placing a checkmark next to them.

The Outline tools are not available for Mac users to add to the toolset. However, the same settings can be accessed on the **Outline** tab of the Properties Inspector.

NOTE: The properties you establish here will serve as the default for graphic objects that you generate in the future if you activate the Outline Pen tool without having an object selected in the drawing window.

To illustrate the Outline tools, we will commence with a straightforward rectangle. Select the **Outline Pen Tool** from the Outline Tools tool group.

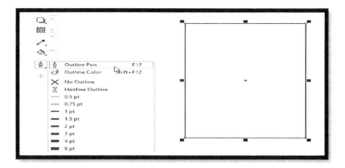

The Outline Pen dialog box will be displayed. The outline color, breadth, and line style can be configured in this location.

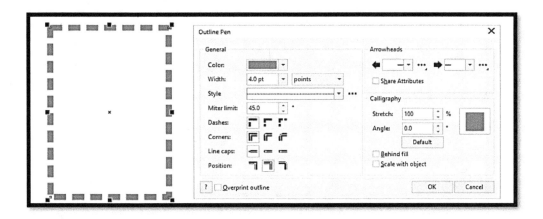

Additionally, there are additional locations within the CorelDRAW interface where outline properties can be modified. The outline color can be altered by right-clicking on a color sample in the Color palette located to the right of the interface, while a solid fill can be added by left-clicking. On the Outline pane, you can modify the line width and design in the **Property Bar** and the **Properties docker/inspector**. The options presented here are identical to those that are accessible in the Outline Pen window.

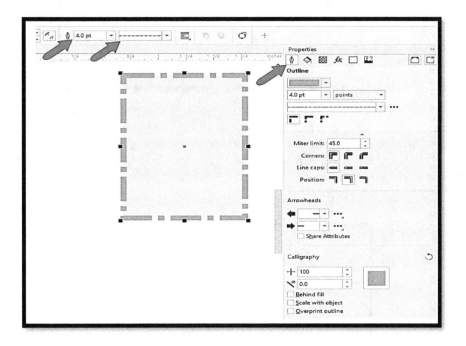

The Outline Pen flyout includes a variety of pre-set line widths. Additionally, you have the option to specify a custom width and various units using the **Properties** docker or the **Outline Pen** window.

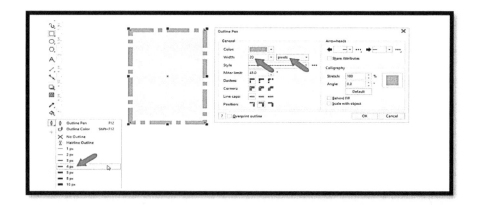

Another method for accessing the Outline Pen window is to double-click the **Outline** swatch in the status bar. If the status bar is not visible for Mac users, navigate to **View > Show Status Bar** to enable the status bar and access the Outline swatch.

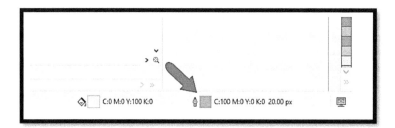

The style settings can be utilized to establish a personalized style when employing a dotted or dashed line style. The repeat distance is determined by the slider, and the repeating pattern is established by filling in the squares to the left of the slider. A new pattern is generated by clicking Add, and it is subsequently accessible in the styles drop-down menu. Alternatively, you can select supplant to supplant the style you initially selected with the new version.

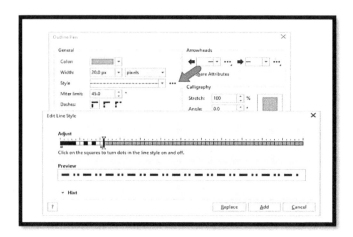

Probably, an outline consisting of dots and dashes will not be symmetrical in either direction. By selecting Align dashes, the style is aligned at the corners, and Fixed Dashes ensures that the dashes are identical at the corners while altering the pattern scale along the margins.

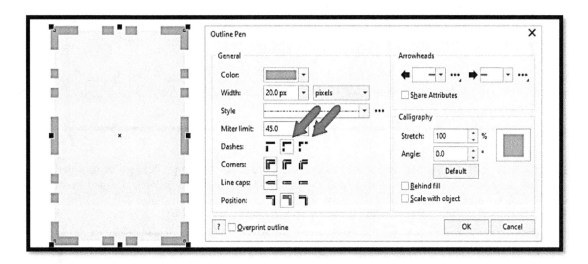

The default line caps have squared edges; however, you have the option to swap to round caps or extended square caps, which extend the length of the line.

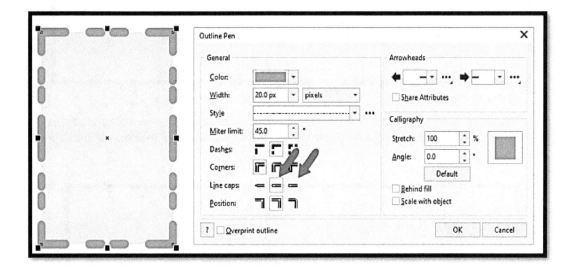

The outline is initially centered with the fill; however, it can be positioned either within or outside the object. A fill can also be positioned behind an outline.

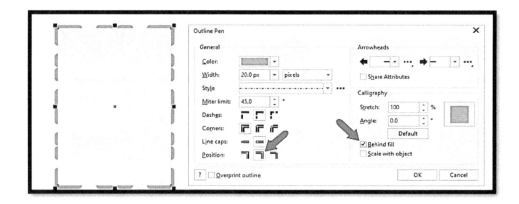

Additionally, corners are pointed or mitered by default. Instead, they may be beveled or rounded. Sharp angles are defined as those that are less than the miter limit for mitered corners. The extremities of a rectangle will be beveled if this angle exceeds 90 degrees.

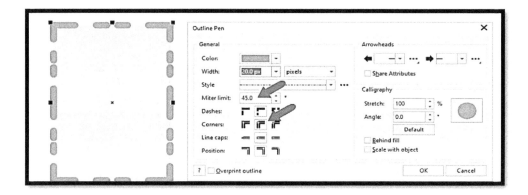

Access the Outline Color tool from the arsenal to achieve more precise control over the color of the outline. In this section, you have the option of selecting from a variety of color viewers or color palettes to fine-tune the values of the colors.

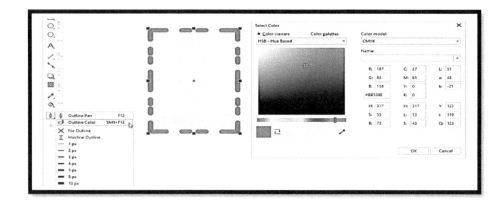

The Pen tool can be used to draw open curves, such as this one, to which outline settings are applicable. Arrowheads or other shapes can be affixed to each end of the curve. The three-dot icon on each arrowhead provides the ability to swap the start and end points, as well as an Edit option for modifying properties such as size or rotation angle.

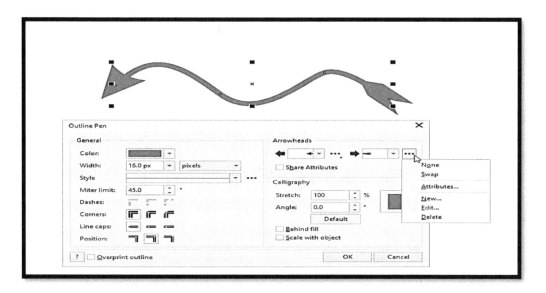

A wide, substantial curve is the most effective way to illustrate calligraphy settings. Adjusting the Angle is equivalent to rotating the nib while decreasing the Stretch value resulting in a hand-drawn pen nib appearance.

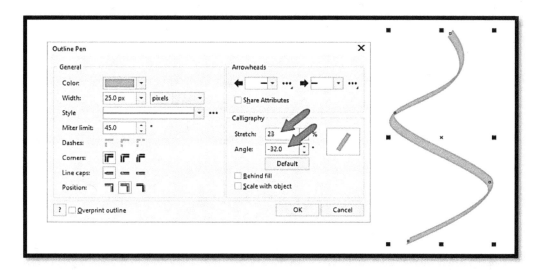

Variations in calligraphy values can also result in intriguing angles and varying thicknesses in non-solid line types.

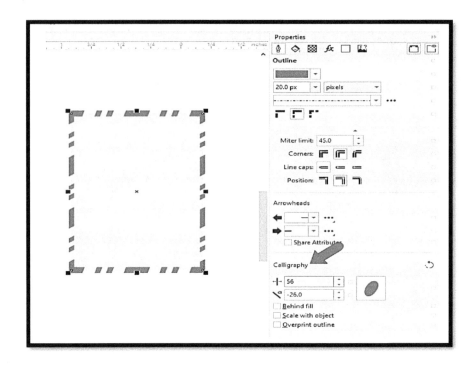

Lastly, the line widths increase as an object is enlarged when **Scale with Object** is enabled.

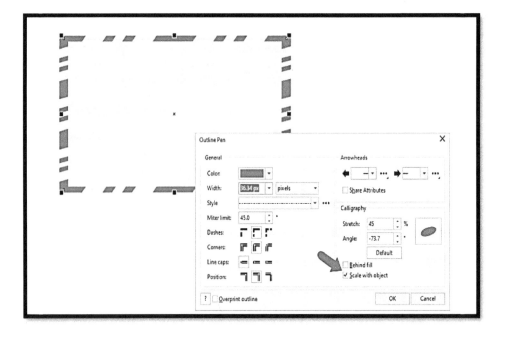

The line widths will remain constant when the object is resized if this option is not selected.

Converting Bitmaps to Vectors

Bitmap to vector conversion is a critical step in graphic design that converts raster images into scalable vector graphics. It is imperative for individuals who utilize image conversion tools such as CorelDRAW to comprehend the distinctions between vector graphics and bitmap images.

The Concept of Bitmap Images

Pixels are the building blocks of bitmap images, which are also referred to as raster images. A comprehensive image is composed of specified color information that is contained within each pixel. JPEG, PNG, and BMP are among the most prevalent bitmap formats. Resolution dependency is one of the primary attributes of bitmap images. This implies that a bitmap image may become pixelated and lose clarity when it is enlarged or zoomed in. This constraint may influence the quality of an image when it is resized for various applications. Complex images with nuanced color gradients, such as photographs, are well-suited to bitmap files. They effectively capture colors and fine details. Nevertheless, this feature is offset by the increased file size, which can be less efficient for online use and storage. This is where vector conversion is advantageous.

Setting Up Your Document for Tracing

Tracing results are significantly influenced by the proper arrangement of documents. Begin by starting a new document and selecting the canvas size that corresponds to the specifications of your project. Make certain that your bitmap image file is prepared for tracing. Import your bitmap image into CorelDRAW by selecting the File menu. When selecting a resolution, it is important to consider the intended output size and strike a balance between efficacy and detail. To ensure that the file remains editable and layers are preserved, save the document in CorelDRAW's native format before tracing. This preparation guarantees the seamless tracing of your vectorized image and assists in the preservation of its quality.

Using the Trace Tool in CorelDRAW

CorelDRAW's Trace Tool is capable of converting bitmap images into vector graphics, providing both precision and flexibility. The following are the fundamental actions and recommendations that will assist in the mastery of this feature.

Accessing the PowerTRACE Feature

Users should initiate the tracing utility by selecting the bitmap image they wish to convert. The **Bitmaps** menu must be opened at the top once the image has been highlighted. The **Outline Trace** option is located in this menu. PowerTRACE, CorelDRAW's integrated tracing utility, is activated by selecting **Outline Trace**. Alternatively, this feature can be accessed by right-clicking on the selected image. PowerTRACE is a valuable tool for the conversion of a variety of images, including technical illustrations and logos.

Choosing the Right Preset for Tracing

To achieve optimal outcomes, it is essential to select the appropriate preset in PowerTRACE. CorelDRAW offers a variety of preset options that are specifically tailored to meet the needs of various duties. Different levels of detail and simplicity are provided in the final vector image by options such as **High-Quality Images** and **Logos**. By selecting **Outline Trace** and then selecting a suitable option from the drop-down list, the user can customize the tracing to meet their specific requirements. This phase accommodates a variety of complexities and details in images. By selecting the appropriate preset, the vector image will closely resemble the original bitmap.

Adjusting Trace Settings Manually

The user can manually modify the settings to enhance the quality of the vector image after selecting a preset. PowerTRACE provides a variety of controls to adjust the precision of corners, flattening, and color detail. The quality of the trace can be improved and specific requirements can be more effectively met by modifying these settings. The final output is significantly enhanced by the fine-tuning of these manual settings, which necessitates some practice. To comprehend the impact of each setting on the image, users should experiment with them. This investigation has the potential to reveal the optimal equilibrium between lucidity and level of detail. Mastering the manual settings in PowerTRACE can substantially enhance the control over the tracing process.

Refining the Vector Output

It is crucial to refine the vector graphic after converting a bitmap to a vector using CorelDRAW's PowerTRACE tool. This process entails the refinement of the ultimate appearance of your design, the management of intricate areas, and the editing of nodes. These procedures guarantee that the output is as near to the desired outcome as feasible and is polished.

Editing Nodes and Curves

After the bitmap has been converted, the vector can be further refined by modifying the curves and nodes. Shapes and lines can be altered by manipulating nodes, which are points on the vector path. In CorelDRAW, the selection of a node enables the manipulation, addition, or removal of nodes, thereby enhancing the precision of curve contouring. A graphic can be rendered more or less fluid or sharp by adjusting contours, contingent upon the requirements of your design. With the shape tool, select nodes and modify the handles to ensure seamless transitions and refine curves. When lines must be precisely aligned or tapered uniquely, this procedure is crucial. Utilize the editing capabilities of CorelDRAW to improve the level of detail in your vector artwork. For example, the design can be more manageable and the file size can be reduced by simplifying nodes, which can expedite complex paths.

Handling Complex Areas and Overlaps

If not managed effectively, complex areas and overlaps can result in a less tidy graphic. CorelDRAW offers tools to address these challenges by facilitating the effortless modification and separation of vector paths. Combine or separate overlapping areas by employing welding or pruning tools. This enhances the vector's visual appeal and equips it for practical applications, such as digital display or printing. It can be beneficial to modify the layering order of layers or objects to simplify tricky areas. Additionally, the separation of compound paths can facilitate the management of complex areas, providing greater control over individual components. This is particularly advantageous in designs that contain numerous intersecting and overlapping shapes.

Applying Final Touches to Your Vector Graphic

It is imperative to incorporate the final details after regulating nodes and intricate areas. Enhance the vector's appearance by employing tints and outlines. CorelDRAW enables you to personalize colors, gradients, and textures, thereby adding a distinctive character to your design. To enhance the dimensionality of the image, it is advisable to implement effects such as highlights or shadows. Another beneficial feature is the conversion of vector strokes to outlines, which can improve the quality of printed materials. The design's intended use should be consistent with the fine details, such as line weights or fill varieties. Unity in the design is guaranteed by the consistent formatting of vector elements. By making these final adjustments, you can enhance the visual allure of your design and ensure that it is available for use.

Creative Uses for Vector Graphics

Vector graphics are the optimal choice for a diverse array of creative applications due to their exceptional scalability and adaptability. These digital images have the potential to improve logo design, create files for a variety of media outputs, and seamlessly incorporate them into larger design projects.

Logo Design and Branding

Vector graphics are indispensable for the development of professional, scalable insignia. Designers utilize them to create emblems that are sharp on both a billboard and a business card due to their ability to be resized without sacrificing quality. This scalability guarantees brand consistency across all platforms. Designers can effortlessly modify colors, shapes, and layouts. Businesses that are striving to establish a memorable and distinctive image will benefit from this adaptability. Companies can guarantee that their branding materials remain consistent and polished as they expand or develop by employing vector graphics.

Preparing Files for Different Media Outputs

Designers frequently encounter the challenge of guaranteeing that their work is visually appealing on both digital and print platforms. This endeavor is simplified by vector graphics. In contrast to raster images, they do not exhibit pixelation when magnified. This attribute is essential for projects that necessitate files that can be adapted to a variety of outputs, including large-scale prints such as banners posters, and web graphics. Designers can effortlessly fine-tune details, alter colors, and experiment with layouts by converting bitmap images into vectors using tools such as CorelDRAW's PowerTRACE. This adaptability guarantees high-quality outcomes across all media formats and saves time.

Incorporating Vectors into Other Designs

Vectors can be incorporated into more intricate design endeavors. They are employed by designers in multimedia presentations, infographics, and illustrations as a result of their adaptability and clarity. This integration enhances the professional appearance and clarity of initiatives. For instance, vector graphics are optimal for architectural diagrams or detailed maps, where precision is paramount. Vectors are ideal for interactive web applications or animations due to their ability to retain their quality when scaled. This adaptability enables them to effectively complement other design elements, thereby improving the final product's functionality and aesthetic appeal.

Troubleshooting Vector Graphics

Challenges may arise, particularly when working with intricate vector projects, even though CorelDRAW is a potent and intuitive tool. Understanding how to identify and resolve these issues, which range from unanticipated design errors to file compatibility and performance issues, guarantees a more efficient workflow and superior outcomes.

Common Issues with Vector Graphics in CorelDRAW

Vector graphic troubleshooting frequently entails the resolution of issues such as file corruption, inaccurate shapes, performance delays, or compatibility errors. The quality of your designs can be compromised and the creative process can be interrupted by these issues. The key to effective troubleshooting is to comprehend the underlying cause of each issue and implement the appropriate solution. Unwanted voids or uneven fills can result from overlapping objects or misaligned trajectories, which are among the most common challenges. For example, when combining multiple objects into a single shape, incorrect welding or pruning may result in invisible openings that become visible during printing. To prevent such issues, it is essential to ensure that objects are correctly aligned and merged. File performance can also be a concern, particularly in larger projects that contain a high number of paths, nodes, and effects. The system can be overloaded by the complexity of the vector graphics if CorelDRAW experiences frequent failures or slowness. Performance can be substantially enhanced by simplifying the design by eliminating superfluous nodes or grouping objects.

File Compatibility Issues

Another frequent area in which vector graphic troubleshooting is required is file compatibility. CorelDRAW accommodates an extensive array of file formats; however, the exportation or importing of files may occasionally lead to data loss or modifications to designs. For instance, the exportation of a complex vector graphic to a raster format such as JPEG may result in pixelation or a loss of precision, while the importation of files from other vector software, such as Adobe Illustrator, may result in missing effects or misaligned elements. Always verify the export and import configurations to resolve compatibility issues. When exporting, it is crucial to choose a format that is appropriate for the intended purpose, such as PDF or SVG, to preserve the vector properties. Use formats such as AI or EPS for importation, and verify that any external resources (e.g., linked images or fonts) are either embedded or available.

Fixing Performance Problems

The complexity of the design is frequently the cause of CorelDRAW becoming slow or unresponsive. Tax System resources can be burdened by files that contain an inordinate number of nodes, layers, or embedded images. One of the most effective methods for resolving this issue is to optimize the file. Begin by streamlining pathways. Utilize the **Shape Tool** to recognize and eliminate superfluous nodes from intricate shapes. CorelDRAW provides the Reduce Nodes option, which optimizes paths without impairing the visual quality of the design. Furthermore, the **Weld Tool** can simplify the process of merging multiple overlapping objects into a single shape. Another essential step in optimizing performance is layer management. To examine and organize your layers, open the **Object Manager Docker**. The file structure can be simplified and performance can be improved by consolidating comparable elements onto fewer layers. Additionally, accidental alterations can be prevented and the system's burden can be reduced by locking or hiding layers that are not presently in use.

Resolving Corrupted Files

When working with vector graphics, file corruption is a rare but aggravating issue. Unexpected failures interrupted saves, or compatibility errors during file transfers can lead to the creation of corrupted files. Start by attempting to access the file in **CorelDRAW's recovery mode** to troubleshoot corrupted files. When the software detects a corrupted file, it frequently prompts you to recover it automatically. If recovery is unsuccessful, attempt to import the file into a new CorelDRAW document rather than accessing it directly. Occasionally, this approach circumvents complications associated with the original file structure. Furthermore, it is possible to utilize your work as a backup in the event of file corruption by storing it in multiple formats (e.g., PDF and CDR) during the design process.

Addressing Design Errors

Occasionally, vector graphics may exhibit unanticipated behaviors, including the rendering of gradients incorrectly, the appearance of irregular strokes, or the failure of objects to fill sufficiently. Improperly confined paths or overlapping objects are frequently the source of these issues. Use the **Shape Tool** to examine the paths for open nodes or unintended overlaps to resolve fill and stroke issues. CorelDRAW offers a **Close Path** option that mechanically connects endpoints, thereby guaranteeing a continuous shape. Verify that the object is entirely closed and does not contain any concealed layers or objects that could potentially interfere with the rendering process if gradients or fills are not displaying correctly. To ensure that the widths and designs are consistent, alter the **Outline Pen Settings** for issues related to strokes. At times, the application of a stroke to a very small object can result in uneven results. To resolve this, the object can be temporarily scaled up to make adjustments and then resized back down.

Troubleshooting Print Problems

Color mismatches, transparency errors, or misaligned objects are frequently the cause of print issues with vector graphics. These issues may arise when designs are not adequately ready for the intended output medium. Always operate in the appropriate color mode to resolve color discrepancies. **CMYK** colors are optimized for printers, so they are preferred for designs that are intended for print. Verify that your document settings are consistent by navigating to **Tools > Color Management**. When exporting designs that contain transparent objects that overlap, transparency issues may occur. CorelDRAW enables the flattening of transparency during export to prevent unforeseen modifications to the output. When exporting for professional printing, it is recommended to adhere to the **PDF/X standard** to guarantee compatibility and maintain transparency settings.

Preventing Future Issues

Adopting best practices during the design process can reduce the necessity for troubleshooting. Regularly storing your work in incremental versions safeguards against data loss and enables you to return to a previous stage if necessary. Enable the **Auto-Save** feature in CorelDRAW to generate backups automatically. Employ a clear and organized workflow by grouping related objects, designating layers descriptively, and eliminating superfluous elements. These behaviors facilitate the identification and resolution of potential problems.

CHAPTER FIVE
TEXT AND TYPOGRAPHY

This section illustrates the process of incorporating both artistic and paragraphic text into a document. After the text has been inserted into CorelDraw, you will acquire the ability to modify text objects, including the ability to modify the characters themselves and alter the fonts and hues. Additionally, you will observe that artistic text can be positioned along a curve, and paragraph text can be accommodated within any closed shape.

Adding and Editing Text in CorelDRAW

Subsequently, you will acquire the ability to generate and modify both artistic and paragraphic text. We will also examine the process of scaling text to suit contours and shapes.

Adding and Editing Artistic Text

The Text tool in CorelDraw allows for the creation of two distinct forms of text: Paragraph and Artistic. Adding artistic text is a straightforward process: simply activate the **Text** tool, select once on the location where you wish to begin the text, adjust the default font or size if desired, and begin composing. By selecting **Enter**, it is possible to incorporate line breaks. The text is completed by clicking on a vacant space.

Once the text has been selected using the Select tool, it is possible to make some standard adjustments, including resizing, moving, or extending in a single direction.
- The text can be rotated by clicking again.
- The text can be sliced and skewn by utilizing the arrows along the sides of the bounding rectangle.
- Select the **Color** option and select a color swatch to modify the text's color.

When the Docker Text is open, navigate to **Window > Dockable windows**. You can accomplish even more. In the **Character** section, you have the option to select a vector fill and select a pattern, or you can experiment with a gradient fill, texture fill, or both. Clicking on the **Fill Settings** button will reveal the fill properties for any of these fill options.

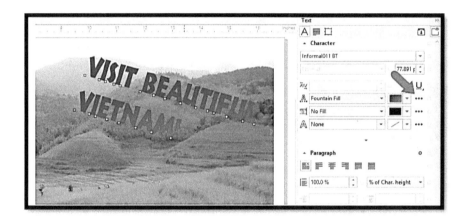

Editing Text Characters in CorelDraw

The characters in a text object can be edited by double-clicking it.

The Text Edit tool is an additional method for editing text in CorelDraw. Type the text and click on it once. Use the settings in the **Property** bar or the **Docker Text** to modify only the characters that you have highlighted by dragging. The kerning, which is the distance between characters, can also be altered when text is selected.

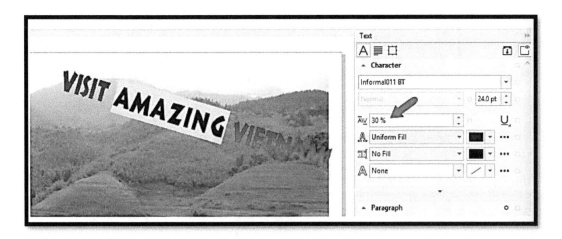

Adding and Editing Paragraph Text

Paragraph text is frequently employed to accommodate substantial quantities of text that are enclosed within a text frame. If you have a limited amount to say, you can manually enter the paragraph text. However, it is typically more convenient to have the text available in another application, where you can access it. First, use the keyboard shortcut **Ctrl + C** to copy the text. Activate the **Text** tool to include paragraph text. The paragraph font settings can be altered either immediately or after the text has been added, as is the case with artistic text. The text frame that will contain the text can be established by clicking and dragging. Then, select **Ctrl + V** to paste the copied text.

While the paragraph text is selected, you have the option to reposition it or utilize the handles to modify the frame's size. Additionally, it is feasible to modify the text properties of the entire frame in CorelDraw. You can, for instance, modify the color of the text to blue.

Alternatively, you can double-click to modify the text and modify only the characters that are currently selected. If the text frame in CorelDraw turns crimson, it means that the frame is insufficiently large to accommodate the entire text. To resolve this issue, select the text once more and expand the frame until it turns blue. The frame was also filled with a background color in this example.

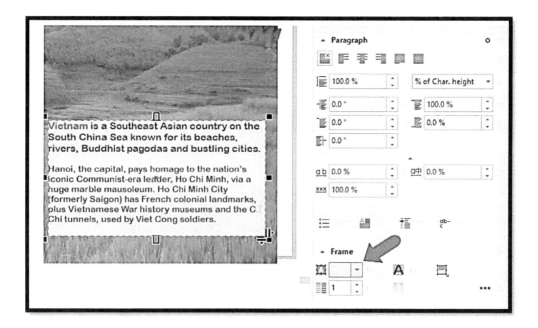

Adding Text to a Path or Curve

With both forms of text, it is not restricted to rectangular boundaries and straight lines. Start by incorporating artistic text into a path. Trace mountain contours by employing the **Bézier** tool, which is located in the movable menu of the freehand tools group on the left toolbar.

Then, select the text and navigate to **Text > Wrap text to path**. Next, position your cursor along the curve and click to make the necessary adjustments. It is still possible to modify the text.

Alternatively, suppose you have a curve but no text. Activate the **Text** tool and move the cursor over the curve until the **cursor icon** transforms into a **curve symbol**.

The text will automatically conform to the curve once you begin typing.

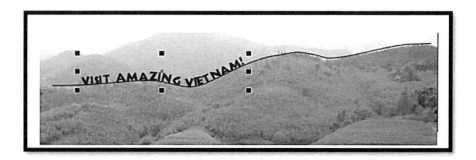

You have the option to scale this text or relocate it by dragging a white square when it is selected. The focal point of the text can be relocated by employing a **red rhombus, or glyph.**

Add Paragraph Text to a Shape

The use of a rectangular frame for your paragraph text is also not required. Any closed shape can be implemented. Draw an ellipse on the page using the **Ellipse** tool, and then use the **Docker Properties** to give it a transparent infill and a wider outline.

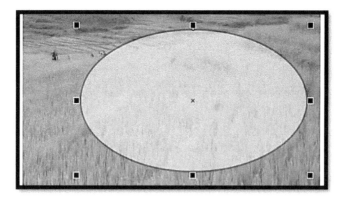

Let us assume that you wish to insert text into an ellipse that is already formatted in a Word document. Before this document can be imported, it must be closed.

Vietnam

A Southeast Asian country on the South China Sea known for its beaches, rivers, Buddhist pagodas and bustling cities.

Hanoi, the capital, pays homage to the nation's iconic Communist-era leader, Ho Chi Minh, via a huge marble mausoleum. Ho Chi Minh City (formerly Saigon) has French colonial landmarks, plus Vietnamese War history museums and the Củ Chi tunnels, used by Viet Cong soldiers.

When the Text tool is enabled, the cursor will display two cursor indicators when it is moved to the ellipse. You will be positioning text along the ellipse's outline if you select the curve icon, as we observed with the **Bezier curve**. However, when a closed shape is identified, the icon transforms into a frame when it is moved slightly inward, indicating that the paragraph text will occupy the shape.

When the frame icon is visible, click. Add text by typing, pasting, or importing. To import text into CorelDraw, navigate to **Archive > Import**. CorelDRAW restricts the search to file formats that support text, rather than image formats, as a result of the fact that you are importing while the Text tool is enabled. Choose the file that contains the text you wish to utilize. Then, you will be presented with the option to retain or abandon the typefaces and formatting of your text document in CorelDraw. Select the desired options and select **OK.**

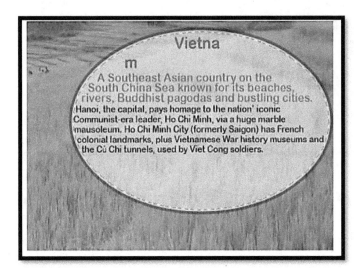

In this instance, the shape is not quite appropriate for the text. Consequently, we will transform the ellipse into a curve by activating the **Selection** tool, right-clicking on the ellipse, and selecting "**Convert to curves.**" Subsequently, we employ the Forma tool to modify the curve's contour, and the text is updated consequently.

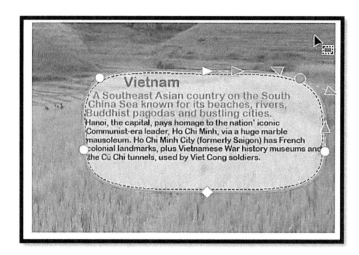

The text can be edited by double-clicking on the frame using the **Selection** tool. In CorelDraw, you have the option to modify the text directly or utilize the **Edit** text window to present it in comprehensible paragraphs. The interactive feature Opentype de CorelDRAW is available to those who utilize OpenType fonts. If you drag to select a character for which there are Opentype alternatives, a small triangle will be visible beneath the character. Some of the stylistic themes that can be used instead will be revealed by clicking on this triangle.

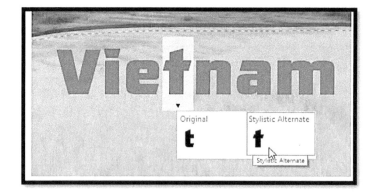

Linking and Combining Text Frames in CorelDraw

We can combine text frames. Additionally, text frames can be subdivided into subcomponents, including characters, words, lines, bullets, paragraphs, and columns. It is possible to click on the text elements either before or after it has been typed. Whenever we alter the text size or resize any linked frame, the quantity of text in the subsequent frame will be automatically adjusted. The cyan arrow indicates the direction of the text flow when an object or text frame is selected. These arrows can be displayed or concealed. We can eliminate the connections between objects and frames, as well as between multiple frames.

Separate and Merge Paragraph Text Frames

To divide and consolidate text frames, implement the subsequent procedures:

1. Select any text frame. To select subsequent text frames, hold down the **Shift** button and employ the **Select** tool when combining any text frame.

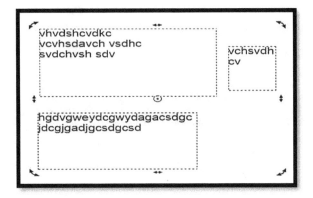

2. Select any of the following by pressing the **Object** button:
   o To combine

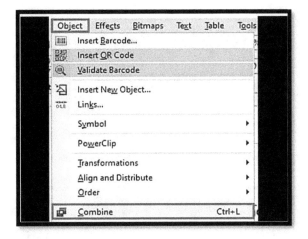

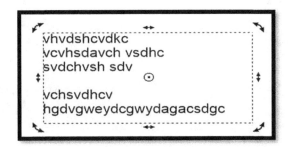

○ Pull apart

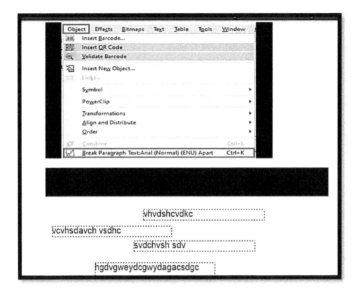

These columns will be present in the combined text frame if we initially select the text frame and the columns.

Align Text Using a Baseline Grid

By employing a baseline grid, it is possible to align text within the frame or between different frames. For instance, this is advantageous when aligning numerous text frames that exhibit disparate spacing, font sizes, and font types. To ensure that paragraph text is in alignment with the baseline grid

The following are the steps:
- Select the **View** option, then navigate to the **Grid** section, and finally, select the **Baseline Grid** option.

- Select the text frame.
- Select **Text > Align to the baseline grid**.

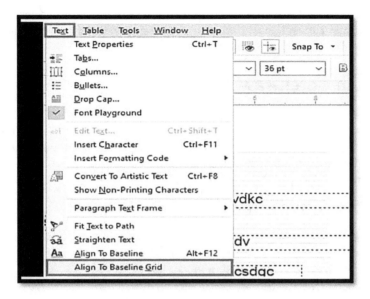

Furthermore, it is possible to right-click on a text frame and select the **Align to Baseline Grid** option. We can align two or more selected frames simultaneously.

Select Text

We can select text in CorelDraw to modify specific characters or modify it as an object. For instance, we can select individual characters to alter the font to select a text object, such as the text frame. Consequently, it is feasible to rotate, resize, or relocate it.

Select the text object in CorelDraw

The following are the steps:
- Select the artistic text by pressing it with the Select tool.
- Select the text frame by pressing it with the Select tool.

In CorelDraw, the Select tool can be employed to select various text objects. To accomplish this, it is necessary to strike all text objects while simultaneously holding down the **Shift** button.

Select the text for editing

The appropriate course of action is as follows:
- Utilize the **Text** tool to navigate the text and select paragraph text or specific artistic media characters for editing.
- Select the text frame to edit by pressing the text frame with the Text tool.

Converting, Editing, and Searching Text in CorelDraw

We can automatically replace text within the document by searching. Furthermore, we can search for special characters, such as a discretionary dash or hyphen. Text can be edited immediately within a dialog frame or drawing window.

Locate a text in CorelDraw

The following are the steps:
- Select **Edit**, and then navigate to Search and Replace, and proceed to **Search text.**
- Enter the text you wish to locate within the text box. To determine the precise case of the text we have described, select the **Match case** checkbox.
- Select **Find text**.

Modify a text in CorelDraw

The following are the steps:
- Select the **Text** tool.
- Involves the execution of any of the subsequent tasks:
  - To modify the artistic text, simply click on it.
  - To modify the paragraph text, click on the text frame.

Also, the dialog box Edit text can be used to make modifications to any text by selecting **Text > Edit text.**

Convert a text in CorelDraw

The following are the steps:
- Select the text and then select **Text > Convert to artistic text** to convert paragraph text to artistic text.
- Select the tool Selection, select the text, and select **Text >> Convert to paragraph text** to convert artistic text into paragraph text.
- Choose the text and select it using the Selection tool. Then, select **Object > Convert to curves** to convert the paragraph or artistic text to curves.

Adding Glyphs, Symbols, and Special Characters

By employing an introduce Character docker, it is possible to introduce and search for glyphs, symbols, and special characters from specific OpenType fonts. The font's characters are classified as follows:
- **Common Equipment:** Includes a variety of symbols, including currency, artistic symbols, mathematical symbols, numerals, punctuation marks, and separations.
- **Deeds:** Supports a variety of scripts, including Cyrillic, Latin, Greek, Hebrew, Arabic, Han, Hiragana, and Katakana with select fonts.
- **Opentype:** Includes a variety of **Opentype** functions that are provided by specific sources, including alternate notation forms, fractions, discretionary ligatures, standard ligatures, and more.

Additionally, the inventory of recently used special characters can be employed to duplicate a variety of characters that are frequently employed. The OpenType features that have been employed and the font attributes of the most frequently applied characters are included in this list. Characters that are no longer required can be eliminated from this list.

Incorporate a distinctive character, symbol, or glyph

The following are the procedures that must be implemented:
- Utilizing the **Text** tool, select the location where we wish to incorporate special characters.
- Select **Text > Insert characters.**
- Navigate to the **Insert Character** option and select a font type from the **Source** selection.
- Double-click the character in the list of characters and glyphs.

If you are unable to locate the desired character, open the character filter list box and select the **Full source** checkbox.

Artistic Text vs. Paragraph Text

Artistic Text vs. Paragraph Text in CorelDRAW 2025 emphasizes two distinct approaches to the addition and manipulation of text in their designs. It is possible to select the most suitable option for your project by comprehending the distinctions between each variety, as each serves a distinct purpose. It is imperative to employ text effectively when creating a brochure, infographic, or logo to achieve a professional and polished outcome.

Artistic Text

CorelDRAW's Artistic Text is intended for brief, significant text elements, such as titles, logos, banners, or ornate phrases. It is an exceptional choice for designs that necessitate dynamic effects or distinctive design due to its ability to accommodate creative manipulation.

Features of Artistic Text

1. **Ease of Manipulation:** Artistic text is capable of being arbitrarily scaled, rotated, skewed, and warped. It can be regarded as a graphic element, which enables you to experiment with its positioning and shape.
2. **Shape and Effect Integration:** CorelDRAW's vector tools are seamlessly integrated with Artistic Text. For example, you can implement effects such as shadows, contours, or distortions to enhance the visibility of the text. It can also follow a path, such as curving along a line or shape.
3. **Character-Based Formatting:** Artistic Text, in contrast to Paragraph Text, emphasizes the formatting of individual characters. It is an excellent tool for inventive typography, as it allows you to modify properties such as font size, color, and spacing for specific characters.
4. **Independent of Bounding Boxes:** The layout of Artistic Text is not determined by a bounding boundary. If you are not concerned with margins or alignment constraints, you are free to position it anywhere on the canvas.

Artistic text is frequently employed for the following purposes:
- **Logos:** Suitable for custom typography and decorative text.
- **Headlines:** Ideal for posters or advertisements that require large, attention-grabbing titles.
- **Callouts:** Effective for brief phrases or annotations in designs.

Paragraph Text

Conversely, paragraph text is employed for extended sections of text, including the body of articles, brochures, and newsletters. It is appropriate for designs that are heavily reliant on structured text due to its sophisticated layout options.

Features of Paragraph Text

1. **Text Flow Control:** The layout of the paragraph text is determined by the bounding rectangle. This feature facilitates the management of substantial quantities of text within a restricted area by automatically wrapping the text to suit the frame.
2. **Advanced Formatting:** CorelDRAW offers tools to regulate paragraph alignment, line spacing, indents, and justification. The text is visually proportionate and simple to read as a result of these features.
3. **Linking Frames:** Text boxes can be linked by permitting paragraph text to propagate across multiple frames. This is especially beneficial for documents that span multiple pages and necessitate a seamless transition from one page to the next.
4. **Supports Styles:** Text styles can be applied to paragraph text, which allows for consistent formatting throughout your design. For instance, you can guarantee uniformity by employing a particular design for body text, subheadings, and headings.

Common Uses of Paragraph Text

- **Brochures:** Appropriate for providing comprehensive product descriptions or company information.
- **Magazines:** Utilized for feature stories and articles.
- **Reports:** Reports are well-suited for structured layouts that contain lengthy text sections.

Key Differences between Artistic Text and Paragraph Text

1. **Purpose**:
    - Artistic Text is for short, decorative text elements.
    - Paragraph Text is for long, structured content.
2. **Layout**:
    - Artistic Text doesn't use a bounding box unless converted or aligned to a shape.
    - Paragraph Text is contained within a defined frame, ensuring text wraps and aligns neatly.
3. **Effects and Manipulation**:
    - Artistic Text is more flexible for applying creative effects like shadows, warps, and transformations.
    - Paragraph Text focuses on maintaining readability and layout consistency.
4. **Text Linking**:

- Paragraph Text can link across multiple frames for continuous text flow, while Artistic Text is independent.
5. **Formatting**:
    - Artistic Text prioritizes character-level formatting for visual impact.
    - Paragraph Text offers advanced paragraph-level formatting for structured designs.

When to Use Artistic Text vs. Paragraph Text

The selection of Artistic Text or Paragraph Text is contingent upon the unique requirements of your project. When it comes to developing a headline or logo that requires attention-grabbing, Artistic Text is the optimal choice. It is the optimal choice for designs in which text functions as a graphical element due to its adaptability and creative capabilities. Conversely, Paragraph Text is more appropriate for designs that contain substantial quantities of text, such as brochures or multi-page documents. Its advanced formatting options and structured layout guarantee that your text is visually consistent, legible, and organized.

Combining Artistic Text and Paragraph Text

Both forms of text will probably be employed in numerous initiatives. For instance, a flyer may include a prominent headline that was generated using Artistic Text, while the body copy is formatted using Paragraph Text. By integrating the two, it is possible to achieve a harmonious equilibrium between functional readability and creative expression.

Working with Fonts and Font Management

Fonts are collections of characters that possess consistent design elements, such as letters, numerals, punctuation, and symbols. A broad spectrum of font formats is supported by CorelDRAW, which includes:
- **TrueType Fonts (TTF):** A versatile and frequently employed font for both prints and web applications.
- **OpenType Fonts (OTF):** Advanced fonts that incorporate ligatures, alternate characters, and stylistic sets, among other typographic features.
- **Type 1 Fonts:** Although they are less prevalent today, they are still utilized in professional publications.
- **Variable Fonts:** A contemporary format that enables the dynamic adjustment of weight, breadth, and other attributes.

CorelDRAW seamlessly incorporates these fonts into your workflow, offering tools to effectively apply, manage, and edit text.

Adding Fonts to CorelDRAW

To utilize a particular font, it must be either installed on your system or administered through CorelDRAW's Font Manager. The process for incorporating typefaces is as follows:
1. **Installing Fonts on Your System:**
    - Obtain the font file (in TTF, OTF, or another format) from a reliable source.
    - For Windows, right-click on the font file and select "**Install**" or for Mac OS, double-click and select "**Install Font.**"
    - If the new font does not appear immediately, restart CorelDRAW.

2. **Using Corel Font Manager:**
    o The Corel Font Manager is a standalone application that is a component of the CorelDRAW Graphics Suite. It enables you to manage fonts without the need to install them on your system.
    o You can evaluate fonts, activate or deactivate them, and organize them into collections. Fonts that have been activated are immediately accessible in CorelDRAW.

Applying Fonts in CorelDRAW

To use a font in your design:
1. To generate text, select the **Text Tool** and click on the canvas.
2. Type your text and highlight it.
3. To select a typeface, click on the font dropdown in the **Property Bar**.
4. Directly from the Property Bar, modify the size, style (bold, italic, etc.), and other properties.

Additionally, CorelDRAW enables you to implement advanced typography settings, including tracking, leading, and kerning, to enhance the visual appeal of your text.

Advanced Font Features in CorelDRAW

1. **OpenType Features:** CorelDRAW can support OpenType fonts, which are characterized by advanced typographic features such as stylistic alternates, fractions, and ligatures. To gain access to these:
    o Highlight the text.
    o Access the **Character Formatting Docker**.
    o Customize your text by adjusting features such as ligatures or swashes.
2. **Variable Fonts:** CorelDRAW's variable font support enables you to dynamically adjust the weight, breadth, and slant of fonts. This adaptability is optimal for the development of personalized typography without the necessity of distinct font files.
3. **Text Effects:** In CorelDRAW, fonts can be altered through the use of effects such as shadows, outlines, gradients, and transparency. These effects seamlessly incorporate your text into your designs and improve its visual allure.

Font Management with Corel Font Manager

It is imperative to maintain a clutter-free workspace and guarantee seamless performance through the implementation of effective font administration. Corel Font Manager provides tools to organize, preview, and activate fonts, simplifying the process of selecting the appropriate typefaces for each project.
1. **Organizing Fonts:**
    o Develop collections to organize fonts by project, style, or category. For instance, fonts can be categorized into collections such as "Sans-Serif," "Script," or "Logos."
    o Tag fonts with keywords to simplify searching later.
2. **Previewing Fonts:**
    o Utilize the **Font Playground** feature in Corel Font Manager to preview typefaces with your personalized text. This facilitates the selection of the appropriate typeface for your design before its implementation.
3. **Activating and Deactivating Fonts:**

- Fonts can be temporarily activated for a specific project and deactivated afterward to conserve system resources. If you possess an extensive font library, this attribute is exceedingly advantageous.
4. **Detecting and Resolving Font Conflicts:**
   - The Corel Font Manager is capable of detecting typefaces that are duplicates or conflicting on your system. By consolidating files or deactivating superfluous versions, these issues can be resolved.

Troubleshooting Font Issues

1. **Missing Fonts:** CorelDRAW will prompt you to replace the missing typefaces if you open a project that employs fonts that are not installed on your system. Utilize the **Font Substitution Dialog** to either replace them or install the necessary fonts.
2. **Slow Performance:** CorelDRAW may experience performance degradation due to an excessive quantity of installed fonts. Enhance performance by deactivating unused fonts with Corel Font Manager.
3. **Font Rendering Problems:** Verify the document's resolution settings if the fonts appear ragged or irregular. Ensure that the resolution is set to a minimum of 300 DPI for print applications.
4. **Compatibility Issues:** CorelDRAW may not display certain obsolete fonts accurately. It is possible to remedy this issue by converting the text to curves (**Ctrl+Q**); however, the text will no longer be edited.

Best Practices for Working with Fonts

1. **Limit Your Font Choices**: Using too many fonts in a single design can create visual clutter. Stick to a maximum of two or three complementary fonts.
2. **Choose Fonts with Purpose**: Select fonts that align with the tone and message of your design. For instance, a serif font conveys tradition and formality, while a sans-serif font appears modern and clean.
3. **Use Font Effects Judiciously**: Effects like shadows or outlines should enhance readability, not detract from it. Ensure that the effects are subtle and support the overall design.
4. **Test Legibility**: Check the readability of your text at different sizes and distances. This is especially important for designs like signage or advertisements.
5. **Keep Fonts Updated**: Periodically update your font library to include modern typefaces and remove outdated or unused fonts.

Creating Text for Print and Web

The purposes of text for print and web are distinct, necessitating unique considerations for each medium. The primary objective of print is to ensure that the text is legible and distinct in a variety of sizes. This is achieved through physical reproduction. Print designs frequently necessitate high-resolution outputs and consistent color fidelity to guarantee that text appears visually appealing and professional on materials such as business cards, posters, or brochures. In contrast, web text is viewed on digital displays, where factors such as screen resolution, device compatibility, and legibility at lower sizes are critical. In contrast to print, where static layouts are the norm, web designs may necessitate responsive text that dynamically adjusts to varying screen sizes and resolutions. CorelDRAW 2025 offers tools to generate and optimize text for both mediums, thereby guaranteeing a seamless design and deployment process.

Text for Print

Detail is of the utmost importance when creating text for print. The text's appearance on paper is influenced by every element, including font selection and layout. The vector-based environment of CorelDRAW guarantees that text maintains its clarity and precision at any scale, a feature that is especially critical for logos, headlines, and other prominent text elements.

    1.   Font Selection for Print

The readability and aesthetic allure of printed materials can be significantly influenced by the font selection. The reader's eye is directed across the page by the small decorative flourishes of serif typefaces, such as Times New Roman or Garamond, which are frequently employed for body text in print. Sans-serif typefaces, such as Futura or Helvetica, are frequently employed for headings and emphasis due to their contemporary, clean aesthetic. The Text Tool and the incorporated Font Playground in CorelDRAW allow you to evaluate the appearance of various typefaces with your content while experimenting with fonts. Ensure that the fonts you select are scalable and perform well in high-resolution outputs.

    2.   Text Size and Readability

Particularly for body copy, print initiatives necessitate meticulous attention to text size. Body text is typically formatted with a font size of 10 to 12 points, while headlines are formatted with a larger font size. CorelDRAW enables you to preview your text at various magnification levels to simulate its appearance when printed.

    3.   Color Settings

The CMYK color paradigm is employed in print materials to facilitate physical reproduction. To prevent discrepancies between on-screen and printed output, it is crucial to set the colors to CMYK when working with text. The **Color Management** tools in CorelDRAW facilitate the application and verification of accurate color settings.

    4.   Resolution and Output

Text intended for printing must maintain its precision at high resolutions, typically 300 DPI or higher. CorelDRAW's vector-based text guarantees that it scales without pixelation. Export your final design in formats such as PDF/X, which are optimal for professional printing and preserve vector data.

Text for Web

Flexibility and screen legibility are the primary considerations for web design text. In contrast to print, where text remains immutable, web text must be adjusted to accommodate a variety of screen sizes, resolutions, and device types. CorelDRAW 2025 offers a comprehensive suite of tools that are specifically designed to produce text that is optimized for digital media.

    1.   Font Selection for Web

Arial and Roboto are examples of sans-serif typefaces that are frequently employed for web text due to their visual clarity on displays. OpenType typefaces are an exceptional selection for web projects due to their compatibility across platforms and advanced typographic capabilities.

CorelDRAW facilitates the experimentation and application of fonts that are optimized for digital use by integrating with web-friendly font libraries such as Google Fonts. This guarantees that the content is displayed consistently on all devices and browsers.

    2.   Text Size and Responsiveness

Web text must be readable on small screens, such as smartphones, and appear composed on larger displays. CorelDRAW enables the creation of text elements with pixel-based dimensions, which guarantees the precision of web layouts. Testing text at different sizes within the software can assist in evaluating its intelligibility on different devices.

3. Contrast and Color

The RGB color paradigm is employed for web applications because it is consistent with how colors are displayed on digital screens. CorelDRAW's **Web Palette** guarantees that your text colors are optimized for online use. Additionally, it is essential to maintain a strong contrast between the text and the background to ensure readability and accessibility. For instance, the utilization of dark text on a light background or the reverse guarantees clarity.

4. File Optimization

Text for the web is frequently exported as a component of vector graphics or images. Formats such as SVG are optimal for text-based designs that require scalability, such as logos or symbols. Conversely, PNG or JPEG are suitable for rasterized text elements. CorelDRAW's export settings enable you to optimize the quality and size of your files to achieve quicker loading times, all while maintaining visual fidelity.

Design Considerations across Media

Although the specific requirements for print and web are distinct, certain design principles apply to both. For the development of professional and proportionate text layouts, it is essential to consider alignment, spacing, and hierarchy. CorelDRAW offers the ability to modify kerning, leading, and tracking to guarantee that your text is visually enticing and evenly spaced. It is crucial to maintain a distinct hierarchy for both print and web. Utilize headlines, subheadings, and body text to direct the reader's attention through the content. You can apply consistent designs to paragraphs in CorelDRAW's **Paragraph Formatting** tools, which simplifies the process of creating structured layouts.

Exporting Text for Mixed Media

CorelDRAW enables the exportation of designs in formats that are compatible with each medium in projects that span both print and web. For instance, it may be necessary for a company's logo to be printed on business cards and displayed on its website. By exporting the text as an SVG for the web and storing it as a vector in CDR or PDF for print, you can ensure that the text remains consistent and of high quality across all platforms.

CHAPTER SIX

UTILIZING COLOR

Color Models: RGB, CMYK, and Spot Colors

Color Models: RGB, CMYK, and Spot Colors are fundamental concepts in graphic design that are essential for attaining the desired visual outcome of their projects. CorelDRAW 2025 provides designers with a comprehensive set of tools to customize their designs for various mediums, including digital displays and print production. This includes the ability to work with these color models. By comprehending the distinctions between these models, you can guarantee that your colors are consistent and precise across all platforms.

RGB Color Model

Digital displays and devices, such as smartphones, TVs, and monitors, employ the **RGB (Red, Green, Blue)** color model. It is an additive color paradigm, which entails the creation of colors by combining red, green, and blue light in differing intensities. White light is generated when these colors are combined at their maximal intensity, while black is produced when all light is absent.

Key Features of RGB

- **Application:** Optimal for digital designs, including digital presentations, social media graphics, and websites.
- **Color Range:** The product is suitable for vibrant, high-contrast designs due to its wide range of colors.
- **File Optimization:** RGB designs are lightweight, which is advantageous for web applications.

Working with RGB in CorelDRAW

- To set your document to the RGB color mode, navigate to **File > Document Properties > Color** and select **RGB**.
- Utilize the **Color Palette** to apply RGB colors to objects. The RGB values can be modified either numerically or by employing a color selector.
- Ensure that your designs retain the vibrancy and clarity of RGB colors by exporting them in digital formats such as **JPEG, PNG, or SVG**.

CMYK Color Model

Print production employs the CMYK color model **(Cyan, Magenta, Yellow, Black)**. This color paradigm is subtractive, which means that colors are produced by subtracting light using pigments or inks. Black (or a very dark brown due to ink limitations) is the result of the maximum intensity combination of all colors. The absence of pigment results in the production of white, which exposes the color of the paper.

Key Features of CMYK

- **Application:** Utilized for the production of packaging, posters, business cards, and brochures.
- **Color Range:** Optimized for precise reproduction with tangible inks, despite a smaller gamut than RGB.
- **Precision:** The final printed output is closely matched by colors in CMYK mode, particularly when working with professional printers.

Working with CMYK in CorelDRAW

- In the same **Document Properties** menu, configure your document to use the **CMYK color mode**.
- Utilize the **CMYK Color Palette** to assign colors to objects. Achieve the desired tone by adjusting the percentages of cyan, magenta, yellow, and black.
- Utilize the **Print Preview** feature before printing to simulate the appearance of hues on paper. Preserve the CMYK values of your designs by exporting them in print-friendly formats such as **PDF/X**.

Spot Colors

Spot colors are predefined, premixed colors that are employed in printing to guarantee the consistent and precise reproduction of specific hues. These colors are frequently employed for branding purposes, where precise color matching is essential, or for special effects such as fluorescent and metallic inks.

Key Features of Spot Colors

- **Application:** Suitable for specialty printing, corporate branding, and logos (e.g., metallic or fluorescent effects).
- **Consistency:** Spot colors guarantee that the printed color precisely corresponds to the intended hue, irrespective of the printing process or medium.
- **Pantone Matching System (PMS):** The most frequently employed spot color system, offering a standardized catalog of colors.

Working with Spot Colors in CorelDRAW

- Utilize the **Color Palette Manager** to access spot colors and choose from libraries such as **Pantone Solid Coated** or **Pantone Solid Uncoated**.
- Directly apply the desired Pantone color to objects to assign spot colors.
- To guarantee that spot colors are maintained during printing, specify them in the **PDF export settings** during the export process.

Differences between RGB, CMYK, and Spot Colors

1. **Color Space:**
   - o   RGB is well-suited for digital displays due to its extensive color spectrum.
   - o   CMYK is optimized for printed media, despite its narrower gamut.
   - o   Spot colors are predetermined and fixed, guaranteeing precise replication of specific tints.
2. **Usage:**
   - o   RGB is intended for use on displays and the web.
   - o   CMYK is used for basic printing.
   - o   Spot colors are intended for specialty print tasks and identification.
3. **Blending:**
   - o   RGB is an additive process that combines light to produce hues.
   - o   The inks used in CMYK are used to subtract light (subtractive).
   - o   Spot colors are applied as distinct, standalone pigments, rather than blending.

Transitioning Between Color Models

It is simple to switch between color models in CorelDRAW; however, it is important to exercise caution to preserve the fidelity of the color.

1. **Converting RGB to CMYK:**
   - o   The lesser gamut of CMYK may result in a duller appearance of colors when converting from RGB to CMYK. To anticipate these modifications, it is crucial to evaluate your design in CMYK mode.
   - o   Utilize the **Color Proofing** feature to simulate the conversion of RGB colors to CMYK.
2. **Converting to Spot Colors:**
   - o   By selecting an object, opening the **Fill Color Dialog**, and selecting a spot color from the palette, CorelDRAW enables you to convert CMYK colors to spot colors.

Tips for Using Color Models Effectively

- **Start with the End Goal:** Determine the color mode that corresponds to the project's ultimate destination. For digital-only designs, utilize RGB, while for print-oriented designs, utilize CMYK.
- **Calibrate Your Monitor:** The final output is more accurately represented on the screen when the color is calibrated accurately, particularly for CMYK designs.
- **Work with Professionals:** If you are working with spot colors or specialized printing, it is important to work with your printer to ensure that the precise requirements and limitations are met.
- **Export Wisely:** Ensure that the export is in the appropriate format for the target medium. PDF/X or TIFF are recommended for print purposes, while JPEG, PNG, or SVG are recommended for web use.

Color Palettes and Swatches

- **Color Palettes:** A color palette is a collection of predetermined colors that are available for use in your endeavor. These colors can be custom-created to meet specific design requirements, transferred from external libraries (such as Pantone), or system-generated (such as RGB or CMYK palettes).

- **Swatches:** Swatches are distinct color samples that are contained within a palette. Each sample denotes a particular color and its corresponding properties, including RGB or CMYK values. Gradients, patterns, or textures may also be incorporated into swatches.

In CorelDRAW, color palettes and swatches function as your visual toolkit, enabling you to rapidly select and apply consistent colors to a variety of objects and designs.

Default Color Palettes in CorelDRAW

To accommodate various procedures and mediums, CorelDRAW 2025 incorporates a variety of built-in color palettes:
- **Default Palette:** Comprises the most frequently employed RGB and CMYK colors.
- **Web Palette:** A digital project-specific tool that guarantees that colors are rendered consistently across all devices.
- **Pantone Palettes:** Offer industry-standard spot colors for branding and print initiatives.
- **Document Palette:** Ensures project consistency by automatically generating a palette based on the hues used in the current document.

Accessing and Using Color Palettes

CorelDRAW offers effortless access to color palettes via the Color Palette Docker, the Color Picker, or immediately from the workspace. **The following is a guide to the effective use and management of color palettes:**
1. **Applying Colors:** Click on a color sample in the palette to apply it as a fill color after selecting an object. To designate the swatch as the outline color, right-click on it.
2. **Customizing Palettes:** To modify an existing palette or establish a new one:
   - Access the **Color Palette Manager** by selecting **Window > Dockers > Color Palette Manager.**
   - Rename the palette, import new palettes from external sources, or add or remove colors.
3. **Creating Gradients and Patterns:** Solid colors are not the sole limitation of swatches.
   You can generate and save gradients, patterns, and textures as samples for future use.
   - Select **Gradient Fill** or **Pattern Fill** by opening the **Fill Tool.**
   - Modify the settings and save the outcome in your personalized palette.

Creating Custom Color Palettes

Custom color palettes enable you to customize the color palette of your design to align with personal preferences, project requirements, or branding guidelines.

Steps to Create a Custom Palette

1. Launch the **Color Palette Manager**.
2. Select **New Palette** and provide a name for your palette.
3. To incorporate colors into the pallet, either select **Add Color** or drag them from the Color Picker.
4. Preserve the palette for future use.

When working with recurring design elements, such as in branding projects, where the consistent use of corporate colors is critical, custom palettes are especially beneficial.

Using the Document Palette

The **Document Palette** is a dynamic feature in CorelDRAW that automatically accumulates the colors utilized in your project. This palette is updated as new colors are added, allowing for a rapid and efficient method of reusing them.

Benefits of the Document Palette

- Guarantees color uniformity within a single document.
- Minimizes the necessity of searching for colors that have been previously employed.
- Facilitates effortless modifications to the color palette of your design.

To activate the Document Palette, navigate to **Window > Color Palettes > Document Palette** and verify that it is visible.

Importing and Exporting Color Palettes

CorelDRAW enables the importation of palettes from external sources and the exportation of custom palettes for use in other applications or projects.

Importing Palettes

- Launch the **Color Palette Manager**.
- Navigate to the desired palette file (e.g., .cpl or.ai) and click **Add Palette**.
- Load the palette into your workspace.

Exporting Palettes

- In the **Color Palette Manager**, choose your personalized palette.
- Click on the **Export Palette** button and select a file format.
- Preserve the palette for future endeavors or to share it with others.

Using Spot Colors and Industry Standards

Spot colors from libraries such as Pantone are indispensable for guaranteeing color precision in print projects. Spot colors are predefined, standardized colors that are combined using precise formulas to guarantee consistent reproduction across various print tasks.

Spot colors can be accessed by the following

- Launch the **Color Palette Manager**.
- Load a spot color library, such as **Pantone Solid Coated**.
- Apply the color you desire to your objects.

Ensure that the spot colors are preserved by selecting the appropriate settings in the Export Options when exporting your print design.

Color Harmonies and Schemes

CorelDRAW includes tools for creating color harmonies and schemes, helping you develop aesthetically pleasing designs with balanced color combinations.

1. **Color Harmonies**:
    - Use the **Color Styles Docker** to create harmonies like complementary, analogous, or triadic schemes.
    - Adjust a base color, and the harmony automatically updates related colors.
2. **Matching Colors**:
    - Use the **Eyedropper Tool** to pick colors from an image or object and save them to your palette.
    - The extracted colors can then be used to build a cohesive design.

Best Practices for Color Palettes and Swatches

- **Limit the Palette:** To preserve a professional and cohesive appearance, adhere to a restricted number of colors.
- **Organize Your Palettes:** Group palettes by project or theme and use descriptive names to facilitate access.
- **Test Color Contrast:** Ensure that the contrast between the text and background colors is sufficient to facilitate readability, particularly in web designs.
- **Save Frequently:** To prevent the loss of your custom palettes in the event of a system shutdown, it is important to save them regularly.
- **Use Color Profiles**: To guarantee that the colors in your palette are accurately translated to printed materials, utilize calibrated color profiles for print work.

Creating Realistic Objects with Mesh Fill

Before commencing the segment, you must comprehend a few fundamental concepts. The initial concept is that all objects that can be drawn are derived from two fundamental shapes: a circle and a rectangle. For instance, an apple is like a circle, whereas a banana is more like a rectangle.

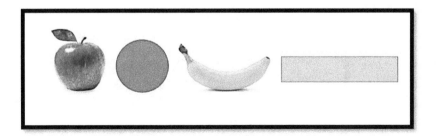

By applying this concept, any object can be reduced to one of the two configurations defined above. An additional notion that requires comprehension is the Mesh Fill tool's functionality. By default, the subdivision operates on both the vertical and horizontal axes.

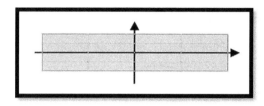

By keeping these concepts in mind, we can generate a straightforward mesh fill that seamlessly conforms to the objects and shapes that require it, and the divisions are effortless to navigate.

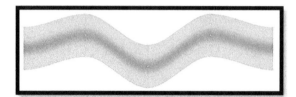

Utilizing an image as a foundation is the most straightforward approach to mastering the Mesh Fill tool. Any image can be employed for this tutorial; however, we will employ this shoe image.

We will now proceed to identify the minor shapes that are present in the image. By deconstructing the illustration into smaller components, you will have greater control over the tool. In our shoe image, we have identified 15 rectangles that we will utilize with the **Mesh Fill** tool. The details will be generated in tiny components using vector objects.

Creating a Mesh Fill Grid

We will commence with area #7, which is the sole of the shoe. Choose the **Rectangle** tool and generate the initial rectangle. The default 2x2 mesh grid will be automatically applied when the **Mesh Fill** tool is activated.

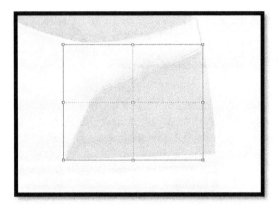

Drag the **Mesh Fill** tool around the mesh you have just created to marquee-select all the nodes while it is still active. To convert all nodes to lines, select the "**Convert to Line**" icon located in the Property bar. This will enable you to more effectively manage the lattice grid's shape. Additionally, in the Property bar, alter the **Transparency** slider to 100 to enable you to observe the object beneath the mesh.

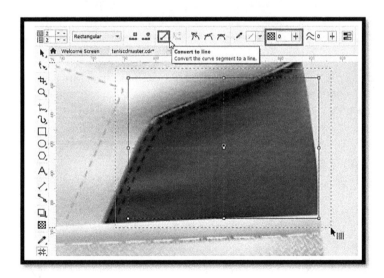

It is now necessary to modify the position of each white node to align with the shape of the area below. It is advisable to maintain the central node close to the object's center, as this will facilitate your work. I have employed color points as a reference to illustrate how I positioned them in the geometry of the shape that I wish to replicate.

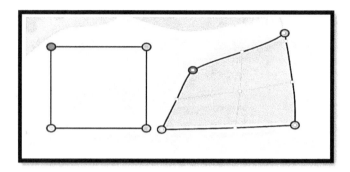

Subsections can be introduced after the mesh grid has been reshaped to correspond with the object area in the image below. The concept is to incorporate new subsections that correspond with distinct colors or shades in the image below. For instance, the darker regions along the left and upper borders, where the stitches are located, are intended to be included.

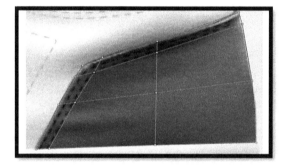

To include a subsection, double-click on the dotted red mesh line to create a horizontal and vertical division in the mesh. Then, coordinate the nodes with the color area below. Continue to incorporate intersections and modify nodes until you achieve a result similar to this.

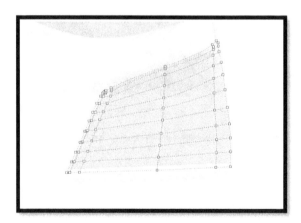

TIP: It is important to remember that each time you double-click; a horizontal and vertical division is created. These divisions are tools in the production of genuine effects; however, it is recommended that the number of nodes be restricted. We will initiate a new object by employing the same method: generating a rectangle, applying a mesh, and adjusting the points to shape the object.

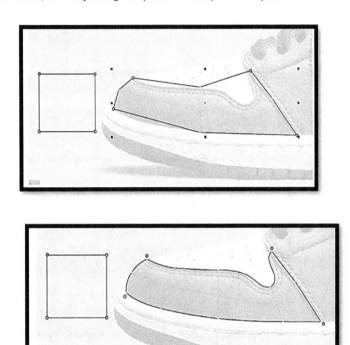

Once the geometry has been established, we can proceed to subdivide and increase the complexity of the mesh grid, resulting in a structure similar to this:

The design will resemble the following once the rectangles have been generated and reshaped to accommodate the objects in the original image:

It is evident that the structure is uncomplicated; however, the application of the lattice grids renders it less so.

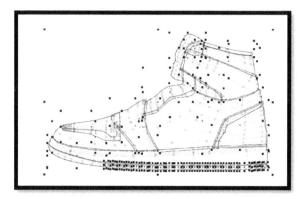

Filling a Mesh with Color

We will now begin to apply color to each object, and this is the moment when the magic begins. The hue of the image will be precisely matched as long as the meshes are created correctly. Select a node or marquee-select a group of nodes that share the same color to add the first color. Click on the **Sample Mesh Fill Color** icon, which is represented by an eyedropper, in the **Property** bar. Additionally, this tool can be initiated by employing the keyboard shortcut **Ctrl + Shift + E**. The **Eyedropper** is used to obtain a color sample that is as near to the node as feasible, ensuring that the precise shade is obtained.

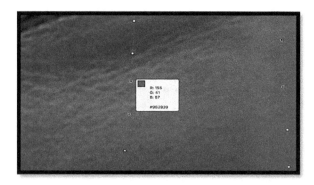

After sampling the color of all nodes in the mesh, we select them all and eliminate the transparency that was applied at the beginning to reveal the mesh color.

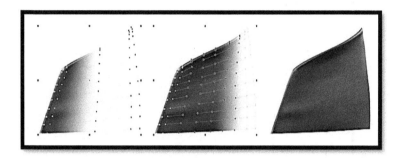

TIP: By activating the **Eyedropper** tool with the command **Ctrl + Shift + E**, time is saved, as the tool is activated and the selected node is automatically copied when the desired color is clicked. Upon completion of the procedure, the final product will resemble this. The sole thing that is lacking is the specifics, such as eyelets and stitching.

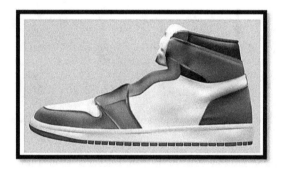

Creating the Finishing Details

The **Bézier** tool will be employed to generate the sutures. Trace the suture line in the original image from point to point. Then, activate the **Shape** tool and select all nodes in the suture line that you have just created. Click on the **Convert to Curve** icon in the Property bar, followed by the **Smooth Node** icon.

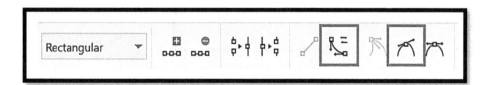

To configure the line appropriately, you can either utilize the Properties docker (**Window > Dockers > Properties**) or open the Outline Pen dialog box by double-clicking on the **Outline** icon in the Status bar. In this section, you can select a line design and modify the width and hue.

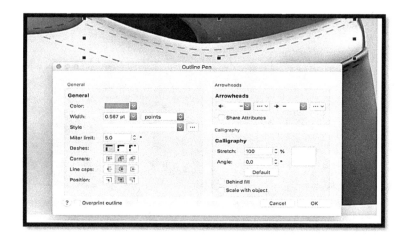

It should resemble the following after all the seams have been added:

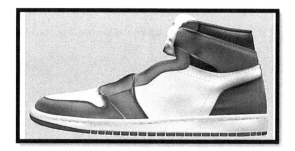

We commence the process of generating the texture pattern on the shoe's sole by utilizing a vector object.

To generate the pattern from this object, navigate to the Transform docker (**Window > Dockers > Transform**), specify the relative horizontal (X) position (8.0) and the number of copies (90), and then select **Apply.** This will generate a single line of vector objects that have been duplicated. Subsequently, establish a relative vertical (Y) position of approximately -16.0 and the number of copies to be used (3). Click **Apply**

once more. Select all lines of duplicated vector objects and group them by pressing the **Ctrl** key and the **G** key. This will provide you with the texture pattern fill.

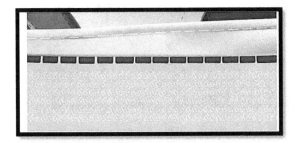

Utilize the **Pick** tool to relocate the texture pattern and subsequently employ the **Envelope** tool to conform the pattern to the sole's contours.

The shoelaces are black objects that have been generated using the **Bézier** tool to create the shape's outline and the **Freehand** tool to generate the brighter patterns within the laces. Black fills the outlined shapes.

A realistic-looking image is the outcome of all those small details when they are finalized.

The **Mesh Fill** tool offers a significant advantage in that it can be seamlessly integrated with other tools, such as the Color Editor or Harmony Editor, to modify the color of the entire image with a mere few taps, as our creation is a vector.

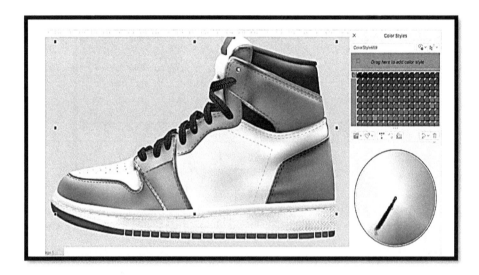

With your comprehension of the process of constructing and coloring mesh fills, you can now commence the creation of your realistic objects in CorelDRAW.

How to Use Color Harmonies

This tutorial will provide a comprehensive overview of color harmonies in CorelDRAW and demonstrate how to rapidly modify the color palette of a project. A harmony is a collection of colors that are organized according to their pigment. When one color in the harmony is altered, the other colors will also be affected. In this instance, I intend to modify the cupcake's color palette to correspond with the café's text. Rather than manually altering each color variation in this graphic, I can employ color harmonies to alter the color palette while preserving the tonal variation.

How to Create a Color Harmony

Initially, it is necessary to access the Color Styles Docker. Navigate to **Window > Dockers > Color Styles** or select **CTRL + F6** on your keyboard. **The Color Styles docker will be displayed on the right. A color style is established by:**

- Choose the group of items that you wish to manipulate.
- Drag them to the section labeled **Drag here** to introduce a color palette and create a harmonious effect.

The dialog box **Create Color Styles** will appear, displaying the color harmonies that have been automatically generated for you. The harmony groups have been categorized according to their color variations.

- Adjust the slider to increase or decrease the number of harmonies you wish to generate.
- Next, select **OK**.

These color harmonies have been incorporated into our Color Styles docker.

Note: Your color harmonies may not be arranged in the manner you desire if you have a complex image. To modify the color palettes:

- Drag the color style onto the harmony that you wish to associate it with.

How to Edit Color Harmonies

- Select the harmony folder that requires modification.
- Choose any of the handles in the **Harmony Editor**. The colors in the harmony will begin to alter as you move the handle around the color wheel.
- The new color palette will be applied to your graphic upon the release of your mouse.
- Repeat these procedures for any color harmonies that require modification.

How to select a specific color and adjust the luminance or darkness levels

- Access the **Color Editor** section located beneath the **Harmony Editor**.
- Utilize the **eyedropper** icon to obtain a sample of the desired color from your design project, which will be incorporated into the color harmony.
- Modify the luminosity or darkness of the hues beneath the color wheel by adjusting the slider.

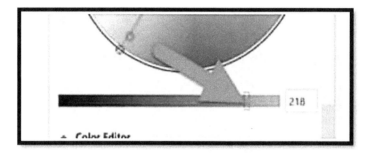

How to Adjust a Color Independently

The handles can be independently moved to alter a specific color style within the harmony, allowing for even greater precision in your color selection. Here, the selector rings are all double rings. By selecting one of them and dragging it, all of them will be moved in "harmony," as we have been doing.

To modify a selector ring without affecting the overall color harmony:
- If you click on one of the selector rings again, you will observe that all of the other selector rings have a single ring. The item that you selected will be a double ring.
- You can now relocate this item independently of the others to the color tone and hue that you prefer, without influencing the other colors in harmony.
- Maintain the original saturation by holding down the **Ctrl** key while dragging the selector ring.
- Hold down **Shift** to preserve the original hue.

The color harmonies feature in CorelDRAW enables you to effortlessly modify the color palette of your designs and illustrations with just a few taps.

Using Fill, Gradient, Pattern, and Texture Techniques in CorelDRAW

The fill tool in CorelDRAW enables the addition of color, texture, or pattern to an object or text. You have the option to select from a diverse selection of predefined fill options or develop your custom fill. To apply a fill, select the object or text you wish to cover and click on the fill tool in the interface. Afterward, you have the option to select the fill type, color, and other settings to personalize your design. Another potent fill effect in CorelDRAW is gradients. They enable you to establish seamless transitions between two or more colors, thereby establishing a sense of depth and dimension in your designs. To apply a gradient fill, select the object or text you wish to fill and click on the gradient tool in the interface. Alternatively, you can generate your custom gradient by modifying the color ends and direction, or select from a variety of predefined gradients. Patterns and textures are also effective methods for incorporating visual intrigue and texture into your designs. CorelDRAW offers a diverse selection of pre-defined textures and patterns that can be applied to text or objects. To apply a pattern or texture, select the object or text that you wish to populate and click on the pattern or texture tool in the toolbar. Subsequently, you can select from the available patterns and textures or incorporate your custom ones. By employing fill, gradient, pattern, and texture in CorelDRAW, you can elevate your designs to the next level. CorelDRAW offers the tools and flexibility necessary to realize your creative vision, whether you wish to incorporate a striking color, generate a realistic texture, or implement a distinctive pattern. Therefore, proceed to investigate these fill effects in CorelDRAW and liberate your imagination!

Understanding Fill, Gradient, Pattern, and Texture Options

CorelDRAW's fill, gradient, pattern, and texture options enable you to improve your designs by applying color, texture, and dimensionality to objects and shapes. **These alternatives provide a diverse array of opportunities for the development of visually enticing artwork.**

- **Fill:** The fill option enables the application of solid colors or even images as the background or interior color of an object. You have the option to select from a diverse selection of pre-set colors or develop your own by modifying the hue, saturation, and luminance settings. This option is beneficial for generating vivid backgrounds or filling shapes with specific hues.
- **Gradient:** The gradient option allows you to apply a gradual combination of colors to an object. The direction, angle, and transition of the color composite can be customized by selecting from linear, radial, conical, or square gradients. Gradients can enhance the depth and dimension of objects by establishing a seamless transition between various hues or tones.
- **Pattern:** The pattern option allows you to populate objects with repeating designs, including polka dots, stripes, or any custom pattern you design. CorelDRAW provides a diverse selection of pre-existing patterns or enables users to generate their own. Patterns are an excellent method for incorporating visual intrigue and texture into your designs.
- **Texture:** The texture option enables the application of authentic surface textures to objects. You have the option of selecting from a diverse selection of predefined textures or generating your custom textures. Textures can enhance the realistic and engaging quality of your designs by imparting a tactile quality.

By comprehending the fill, gradient, pattern, and texture options in CorelDRAW, you can elevate your designs to the next level by incorporating visual interest, dimension, and depth.

Step-by-Step Guide: Applying Fill, Gradient, Pattern, and Texture in CorelDRAW

1. CorelDRAW is graphical design software that enables the creation of exceptional artwork. CorelDRAW's capacity to incorporate a variety of textures, gradients, patterns, and fills into your designs is one of its most significant capabilities. We will guide you through the process of applying various fill effects to your artwork in CorelDRAW in this step-by-step guide.
2. Open CorelDRAW and either create a new document or access an existing one.
3. Choose the text or object to which you wish to apply the fill effect.
4. To access the **Fill** interface, either selects the **Fill** utility from the toolbar or press the **F11** key.
5. The **Fill** panel contains a variety of options for applying fill effects. Begin by performing a fundamental fill. Select the **Uniform fill** option.
6. Select a color for the fill from the color palette or manually input the RGB or CMYK values.
7. To incorporate gradient effects into your fill, select the **Gradient fill** option.
8. Choose the gradient type you wish to implement, including linear, radial, or conical.
9. Customize the gradient effect by adjusting the colors and position of the gradient ends.
10. Click on the **Pattern fill** option to incorporate a pattern fill.
11. Select a pattern from the library that is currently available or import your pattern.
12. Modify the pattern fill's scale, angle, and other settings to accommodate your design.
13. To apply a texture to your fill, select the **Texture fill** option.
14. Choose a texture from the texture library or import your texture image.
15. Achieve the desired effect by adjusting the opacity and other settings of the texture fill.

16. By applying multiple fill layers to your object or text, you can also combine various fill effects.
17. Utilize a variety of settings and combinations to generate visually appealing and distinctive fill effects.
18. Once you are content with the fill effect, you can further improve your design by modifying other properties, including transparency, blending modes, and outlines.
19. Lastly, save your artwork in the format you prefer and distribute it to others.

Applying fill, gradient, pattern, and texture effects to your designs in CorelDRAW is effortless when you adhere to these comprehensive instructions. Engage your imagination and create distinctive designs!

Exploring Advanced Techniques: Creating Custom Fills, Gradients, Patterns, and Textures

When it comes to the creation of custom fills, gradients, patterns, and textures, CorelDRAW provides a multitude of tools and options to unleash your creativity. By experimenting with these sophisticated methods, you can enhance the depth, dimension, and individuality of your designs. Let us delve into the process of developing our personalized elements. The Interactive Fill utility is one method of generating custom fillings. This utility enables the application of fill effects, including linear, radial, conical, and square gradients, as well as pattern fills and texture fills. Stunning visual effects can be achieved by experimenting with various color combinations, angles, and transparency levels. The Pattern Fill tool is an option for those who wish to generate designs that are more intricate and complex. By drawing a small section and automatically replicating it across the object or page, this tool allows you to create seamless patterns. You have the option to select from a diverse selection of pre-existing patterns or to develop your own by combining various shapes, lines, and colors. The Texture Fill tool is the optimal choice for individuals who wish to incorporate a realistic and tactile quality into their designs. It enables you to imbue your objects with a variety of textures, including wood, metal, and fabric. You can impart a sense of depth and texture to your designs by modifying the scale, rotation, and intensity of the texture. The Gradient Fill tool is an additional potent tool for the development of distinctive elements. CorelDRAW provides a variety of sophisticated gradient options, such as multi-color and fountain fills, in addition to the standard linear and radial gradients. These sophisticated gradient effects enable you to generate seamless transitions between various colors, thereby imbuing your designs with a polished and professional appearance. It is imperative to experiment and investigate various combinations when working with custom fills, gradients, patterns, and textures. Do not hesitate to experiment with a variety of colors, shapes, and effects to generate genuinely unique designs. It is important to utilize the layers feature to separate and organize various elements, which will facilitate their subsequent editing and manipulation. In summary, CorelDRAW offers a wide variety of tools and options that can be used to design custom fills, gradients, patterns, and textures. You can elevate your designs to a new level by experimenting with various combinations and investigating these advanced techniques. Therefore, feel free to discharge your creativity and allow your imagination to soar!

Enhancing Your Designs: Tips for Using Fill, Gradient, Pattern, and Texture in CorelDRAW

The utilization of fill, gradient, pattern, and texture in CorelDRAW can significantly enhance the development of captivating designs. Your artwork can be elevated from ordinary to extraordinary by incorporating these features, which can contribute to its professionalism, interest, and profundity. This article will offer you a variety of tips and techniques to help you optimize the capabilities of these tools and improve the quality of your designs.

1. **Experiment with Different Fill Types:** CorelDRAW provides a diverse selection of fill varieties, such as solid colors, gradients, patterns, and textures. Do not hesitate to explore various alternatives to achieve the desired outcome. Patterns can add interest and repetition, gradients can add dimension and depth, solid colors can provide an assertive and clear look, and textures can bring a realistic and tactile feel to your designs.

2. **Combine Fill Types for Unique Effects:** Do not restrict yourself to utilizing a single fill variety. Unique and captivating effects can be achieved by combining various fill varieties. For instance, visual interest can be enhanced by employing a gradient fill as a foundation and then overlaying it with a pattern or texture fill. Experiment with various combinations to determine the optimal equilibrium for your design.

3. **Modify the Blending Modes and Transparency:** When utilizing CorelDRAW's fill, gradient, pattern, and texture tools, transparency and blending modes can be highly effective. Blending modes can enhance the intricacy and depth of your designs while adjusting the transparency of fill can produce a subtle or dramatic effect. Experiment with various settings to observe their interactions with the fill types you have selected.

4. **Use Color Harmonies:** CorelDRAW offers color harmonies to assist in the selection and application of cohesive color palettes to your designs. Color harmonies can guarantee that your outlines, gradients, patterns, and textures are in perfect harmony. This will lead to a design that is more visually enticing and well-balanced.

5. **Customize and Create Your Patterns and Textures:** Although CorelDRAW provides a diverse array of pre-existing patterns and textures, there is no reason not to create or modify your own. By incorporating a personal touch, your designs can be more distinctive and customized to meet your specific requirements. Utilize the tools and options offered by CorelDRAW to generate textures and patterns that are an ideal match for your designs.

By adhering to these guidelines and comprehending the utilization of fill, gradient, pattern, and texture in CorelDRAW, you can elevate your designs to the next level. Play around, experiment, and allow your imagination to soar. The opportunities are limitless!

Color Profile Management for Printing

Color profiles are standardized collections of data that specify how colors are represented in various devices and mediums, including printers, monitors, and cameras. To preserve uniformity, these profiles translate color information across devices. The **CMYK (Cyan, Magenta, Yellow, and Black)** color model is the most frequently employed color profile for printing, as it is the standard for tangible printing procedures.

- **RGB Profiles:** Utilized for digital displays and screens. They provide a diverse array of colors; however, they are not primarily suitable for printing.
- **CMYK Profiles:** Utilized in the production of printed materials. To precisely reproduce colors, they simulate the way inks will blend on paper.
- **ICC Profiles:** International Color Consortium (ICC) profiles are standardized profiles that facilitate the management of colors across devices, thereby guaranteeing consistency from screen to print.

Why Color Profile Management Is Important

1. **Color Accuracy:** The absence of appropriate color profiles may result in discrepancies between the digital and physical versions of your design, as the printed output may not accurately reflect the intended colors.
2. **Consistency across Devices:** Profiles guarantee that colors appear uniformly regardless of the paper type, printer, or monitor involved.
3. **Optimized Print Results:** The color reproduction capabilities of various printers and substrates (e.g., glossy paper, and matte paper) are distinct. To optimize print quality, profiles accommodate these variations.
4. **Efficient Workflow:** Proper color management reduces material waste and saves time by minimizing trial and error.

Setting Up Color Profiles in CorelDRAW

CorelDRAW 2025 simplifies the process of establishing and maintaining color profiles for printing. This is the method to be followed:
1. **Access Color Management Settings:**
   - To configure global settings for all documents, navigate to **Tools > Color Management > Default Settings.**
   - To establish profiles for individual documents in specific projects, navigate to **Tools > Color Management > Document Settings**.
2. **Choose the Right Color Profile:**
   - Choose a CMYK profile that is compatible with the specifications of your printer or print service for printing. Profiles that are frequently encountered include:
     - **US Web Coated (SWOP):** Used for commercial printing in North America.
     - ISO Coated v2 Used in Europe for offset printing.
     - **Japan Color:** The standard for Japanese printing.
3. **Set Input and Output Profiles:**
   - **Input Profiles:** These profiles specify how CorelDRAW interprets colors from external sources, such as scanners or cameras.
   - **Output Profiles:** Establish the method by which colors are translated for your printer. Utilize the ICC profile that was supplied by the manufacturer of your printer or the print service you are using.
4. **Enable Soft Proofing:**
   - Soft proofing adjusts the on-screen display to simulate the appearance of colors on paper. Navigate to **View > Proof Colors** to activate it. To preview the printed result, select your printer's profile.
5. **Calibrate Your Monitor:**
   - Calibrate your monitor with tools such as a colorimeter to guarantee that the colors displayed on your screen are as precise as possible. This minimizes the disparity between the colors on the screen and those on the printed page.

Optimizing Colors for Printing

1. **Convert Colors to CMYK:**

- The gamut of RGB colors is broader than that of CMYK, which means that certain RGB colors cannot be reproduced in print. To mitigate disruptions, it is recommended that all colors be converted to CMYK before printing.
- In CorelDRAW, select your objects, navigate to **Edit > Find and Replace > Replace Colors**, and convert them to CMYK.

2. **Use Spot Colors for Precision:**
   - Spot colors, such as Pantone, offer precise color matching for specialty printing or branding. Utilize the **Color Palette Manager** to incorporate Pantone colors into your project.

3. **Check Black Settings:**
   - Utilize a combination of CMYK values (e.g., C: 60%, M: 40%, Y: 40%, K: 100%) in place of unadulterated black (K: 100%) to achieve rich blacks in printing. This guarantees a black that is more vivid and profound.

4. **Avoid Over-Saturation:**
   - Smudging or inconsistent printing may result from excessive ink consumption. Utilize CorelDRAW's **Preflight Tool** to evaluate ink coverage levels and make any necessary adjustments.

Exporting for Print

It is essential to export your design accurately to maintain color accuracy when it is prepared for printing.

1. **Choose the Right Formats:**
   - For professional publishing, utilize **PDF/X** formats (e.g., PDF/X-1a or PDF/X-4). These formats guarantee compatibility with the majority of printers by incorporating color profiles.

2. **Embed Color Profiles:**
   - Ensure that the selected color profile is embedded in the file during export. This enables printers to accurately reproduce the colors.
   - Navigate to **File > Export > PDF**, select **Settings**, and enable the option to embed the ICC profile.

3. **Flatten Transparency:**
   - Printing complications may result from transparent components. Select the appropriate option in the PDF settings to flatten transparency during export.

Working with Print Service Providers

It is frequently necessary to adhere to the specific guidelines for file preparation and color profiles when working with a professional print service. To guarantee optimal outcomes and seamless communication:

1. **Request Printer Profiles:** Request the ICC profiles of your print service. Ensure that your designs are following the printing standards of CorelDRAW by importing these profiles.
2. **Perform Test Prints:** Request a test print or proof from your printer before committing to a large print run. This enables you to confirm the veracity of the color and make any necessary modifications.
3. **Communicate Spot Color Needs:** Verify with the printer that they support the specific pigments used in your design, such as metallics or fluorescents, if they employ spot colors.

Common Challenges and Solutions

1. **Color Shift:**
   - ○ **Problem:** The colors appear to be different in print than they are on the screen.
   - ○ **Solution:** Enable gentle proofing in CorelDRAW and use calibrated monitors.
2. **Out-of-Gamut Colors:**
   - ○ **Problem:** The CMYK color space is unable to reproduce specific RGB hues.
   - ○ **Solution:** Employ the **Color Proofing Docker** to detect and modify out-of-gamut colors.
3. **Ink Coverage:**
   - ○ **Problem:** Smudging or drying issues are the result of excessive ink coverage.
   - ○ **Solution:** For the majority of printers, restrict the total ink coverage to approximately 300%.

Eyedropper

CorelDRAW offers a variety of tools and features for the selection of colors, such as color viewers, palettes, and Eyedropper tools. The **Color Eyedropper** and the **Attributes Eyedropper** are the two Eyedropper tools that will be examined in this tutorial.

The Color Eyedropper

Use the **Color Eyedropper** to obtain an exact color match by sampling a color in a drawing, on a palette, or your desktop.

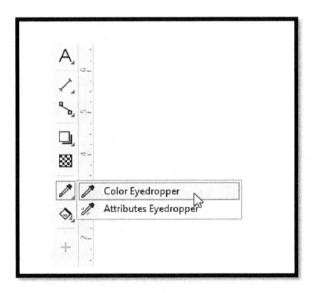

The rectangle outlines in this example will be colored using the hues from the image of the rose, and a solid fill will be applied to the page. Upon activating the **Color Eyedropper** tool, the color values will be displayed as you move the cursor around, depending on the object properties.

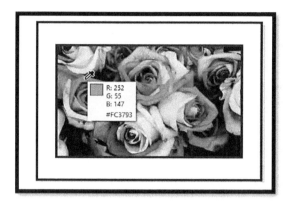

By default, the cursor detects the color of each pixel. However, the property bar contains indicators that can be selected to sample the average color of a 2x2 or 5x5 pixel area.

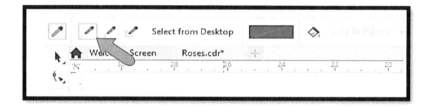

It is possible to modify the ranges by hovering over the various boundaries of the highlighted range on the color wheel, which will reveal white borders. If your cursor is over an outline when you apply a color, the outline symbol will be added to the cursor. Similarly, a solid square will be added to the cursor when using a fill area. The solid overlay is implemented by clicking within the page frame.

Press and hold the **Shift** key to sample an additional color, and the cursor will revert to an eyedropper. Additionally, you can return to the eyedropper by selecting the **Select Color** icon in the Property bar. Choose a new color and, instead of immediately applying it, select **Add to Palette**. This adds the new color swatch to the Document palette, which is located at the bottom of the interface.

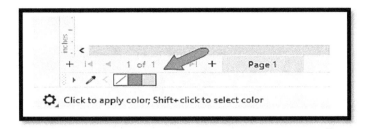

Click to apply color; Shift+click to select color

NOTE: If you have other palettes displayed, you can also select one of them from the **Add to Palette** dropdown.

If the **Document** palette is not visible for Mac users, navigate to **Window > Color Palettes > Document Palette.** In the **Document** palette on the PC, there is also an eyedropper that functions similarly to the **Color Eyedropper**, but it can be utilized while any tool is active.

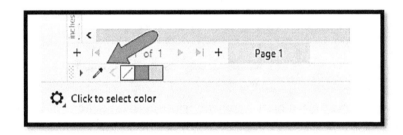

Click to select color

For instance, by transitioning to the Pick tool, you can select a color by clicking the eyedropper in the **Document** palette, and the color will now be displayed in the **Document** palette. **TIP:** While any tool is active, colors in the **Document** palette or any palette along the right side can be directly dragged onto an outline or into a fill.

Sampling Colors from the Desktop

The **Select from Desktop** option is also available in the **Color Eyedropper**, which allows users to select a color from a source outside of CorelDRAW, such as a web page or document. For instance, if you have an image in a Word document and have configured your desktop to allow you to view both applications, you can select "**Select from Desktop**" and then sample the hue from Word. This new color is now prepared for application or inclusion in the document palette. The document palette eyedropper can also sample colors from sources outside of CorelDRAW for PC users.

Color Sampling from Other Tools

The **Color Window** viewer, which is present in numerous locations throughout the CorelDRAW interface, can also be used to perform color sampling. For instance, to adjust the color of text to match another color, you can right-click on the text and select **Properties**. This will display the Properties docker, or **Properties** inspector on the Mac. Click the **Fill Color** swatch on the Character pane of the Properties docker to open the **Color Viewer**. Utilize the eyedropper to customize the text fill color. This eyedropper is also capable of sampling hues from the desktop.

The Attributes Eyedropper

The **Attributes Eyedropper** is employed to replicate a variety of attributes from a single object, including properties, transformations, and effects, and apply them to other objects. This straightforward illustration comprises a rectangle with a gradient fill and an irregular red outline, as well as several other shapes with distinct fills and outlines.

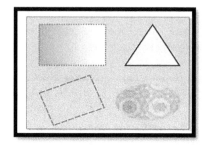

Use the **Properties** submenu on the property bar to select the properties to copy after activating the **Attributes Eyedropper** tool. In this example, the properties to replicate are Outline and Fill.

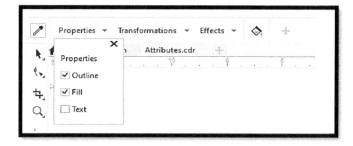

Then, sample the object whose properties you wish to replicate, which in this case is the gradient rectangle.

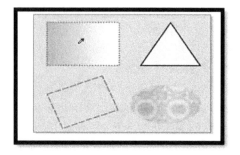

After sampling, you can apply the outline and fill properties to the other shapes.

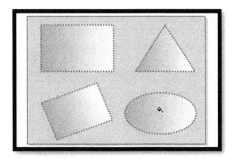

Text properties are also copied and applied by this utility.

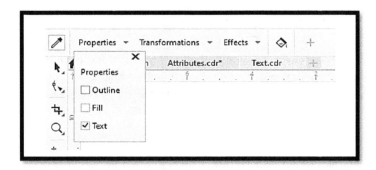

The **Holiday** text was sampled in this example, and its font and size were applied to the other two terms. To replicate all properties, it would be necessary to include **Outline** and **Fill**. Additionally, to replicate the **Contour** and **Shadow** effects from the "Holiday" text, you would incorporate them into the Effects dropdown menu.

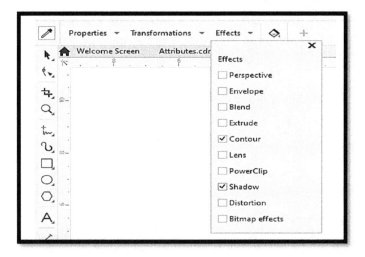

The text objects possess identical properties when all of these properties are selected.

In this example, the only properties that we replicated are **Size** and **Rotation** in the **Transformations** drop-down menu. Following the application of properties to the other objects and the sampling of the rotated heart, they all possess the same dimension and rotation angle. The **Position** option in the **Transformation** drop-down menu can be used to relocate an object so that its center aligns with the center of the sampled object.

Attribute Sampling from Other Tools

Here is an additional method for copying attributes from one object to another. While any other tool is active on the PC, it is possible to right-click on an object and transfers it to another object. The cursor will turn into a target symbol.

You have the option to copy the fill, outline, or all properties from the source object to the target when you release the cursor trigger.

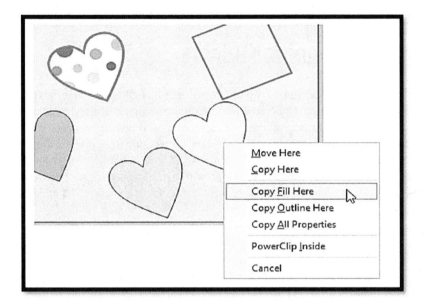

With the knowledge of how to utilize the **Replace Colors** filter in CorelDRAW and PHOTO-PAINT, you can experiment with it today to observe the ease with which it is possible to alter images with greater precision and control.

CHAPTER SEVEN

ADVANCED EFFECTS AND STYLES

PowerClip and Clipping Objects

PowerClip is a feature that enables the insertion of any object, including an image, vector shape, or group of objects, within a container object. The container functions as a mask, displaying only the portion of the content that is contained within its boundaries. This feature is non-destructive, which means that you can modify the contents of the container without irreversibly altering the original objects. PowerClip is frequently employed to generate artistic compositions, logos, and marketing materials. For example, it is possible to embed an image within a text object, a logo within a shape, or a pattern within a custom design. PowerClip is an essential tool for both novice and experienced designers due to its adaptability.

How PowerClip Works

The container and the content are the two primary components of the PowerClip process. The container is the object that establishes the visible boundary, while the content is the object or objects that are inserted within it. **To use PowerClip:**
1. Choose the object (content) that you wish to clip.
2. Navigate to the **Effects** menu and select **PowerClip > Place inside Frame**.
3. The content will be positioned within the boundaries of the container object by clicking on it.

The content conforms to the container's shape once it is contained within it. For instance, the image is cropped in a circular pattern when it is enclosed within a circle. This process is dynamic, enabling the content or container to be modified at any point.

Editing PowerClip Objects

PowerClip's non-destructive modifying capability is one of its most significant advantages. The contents or container of a PowerClip can be readily modified after it has been created.
1. **Content Accessibility:** To edit the content within a PowerClip, right-click on the container and select "**Edit PowerClip**." This launches the PowerClip in an isolated editing mode, allowing you to relocate, resize, or substitute the content.
2. **Exiting Editing Mode:** To exit the editing mode and return to your primary design, select the **Finish** icon or press **Ctrl+Enter** after your adjustments are finished.
3. **Repositioning Content:** The **Pick Tool** can be employed to transfer the content within the container if the content requires adjustment without the need to enter the editing mode.
4. **Customizing the Container:** The container object may also be modified. For example, you can modify its form by converting it to curves **(Ctrl+Q)** and modifying its nodes with the **Shape Tool**.

Applications of PowerClip

PowerClip is an exceptionally adaptable feature that is employed in a variety of design scenarios:
- **Text Effects:** The incorporation of images or patterns within text results in the creation of visually appealing logos or headlines. For instance, you can incorporate a photograph into a robust font to enhance the texture and substance of your text.

- **Masks and Overlays:** PowerClip enables the application of masks by restricting objects to specific regions, such as a shape or outline. This is beneficial for generating overlay effects or guaranteeing that patterns are in perfect alignment with the design's boundaries.
- **Complex Compositions:** Designers employ PowerClip to integrate numerous objects into intricate compositions. For instance, the incorporation of a landscape photograph into a custom illustration can generate an impressive visual impact.

Clipping Objects vs. PowerClip

Although PowerClip is a distinct feature of CorelDRAW, the term "clipping objects" encompasses the more comprehensive process of concealing content within boundaries. The process of clipping in vector graphics typically entails the definition of the visible area of one object by utilizing the geometry of another. This process is dynamically implemented by CorelDRAW through PowerClip, which offers supplementary control and flexibility. While other software may necessitate the permanent merging of objects, CorelDRAW's PowerClip is non-destructive; enabling alterations to be made even after the clipping has been applied. This distinction provides CorelDRAW with a substantial advantage in terms of maintaining the flexibility of its design.

Advanced Techniques with PowerClip

1. **Using Nested PowerClips:** Nested PowerClips can be generated by enclosing a PowerClip within another PowerClip. This method is optimal for the development of multi-level compositions or layered effects.
2. **Combining with Transparency**: To accomplish subtle overlays and blending effects, add transparency to the PowerClip container or its contents. For example, a semi-transparent pattern can be generated within a custom shape to produce a distinctive background effect.
3. **Working with Gradients and Patterns:** Clipping gradients, patterns, or textures into objects enables the application of custom fillings that are following the container's geometry. This is especially advantageous in the context of branding and decorative designs.
4. **Dynamic Updates:** The content can be dynamically updated due to the non-destructive nature of PowerClip. For instance, when an image is replaced within a PowerClip container, the new image is automatically adapted to the container's geometry.

Tips for Effective Use of PowerClip

- **Plan your Layers:** Plan your layers and objects before applying PowerClip. To facilitate editing and guarantee that your design remains manageable, organize elements that are related.
- **Use Snap Tools:** Enable the attaching to objects, guidelines, or grids to guarantee the precise positioning of PowerClip contents.
- **Experiment with Shapes:** Do not restrict yourself to fundamental shapes as containers. Utilize custom shapes, paths, or even hand-drawn objects to achieve unique effects.
- **Test Printing:** When preparing a print design, verify that the clipped content is aligned correctly with the container and that no unanticipated edges or artifacts appear.

Troubleshooting PowerClip Issues

1. **Content Visibility:** To reposition or resize the content within the container if it does not align as anticipated right-click on the container and select **Edit PowerClip**.
2. **Container Edges:** Guarantee that the margins of the container are well-defined and sleek. If necessary, convert the container to curves to enhance its form.
3. **Exporting PowerClip Designs:** When exporting PowerClip objects, select a format such as PDF or PNG that maintains the design's integrity. Verify the export settings to guarantee that the trimmed content remains within the container's boundaries.

Transparency and Blending Modes

Transparency is the capacity to render an object partially or wholly transparent, thereby enabling the objects or background beneath it to be observed. This can be applied to shapes, images, text, or any object in CorelDRAW, and it is precisely controlled to produce a diverse array of effects, including gentle overlays, gradients, and subtle blending.

Applying Transparency

To implement transparency:
1. Choose the object that requires modification.
2. Select the **Transparency Tool** from the toolbox.
3. Transparency can be established by clicking and dragging the object. The gradient of transparency is determined by the direction and duration of the drag.
4. Utilize the **Property Bar** to regulate the transparency level, which offers numerical input or sliders for precise control.

There are numerous methods by which transparency can be implemented:
- **Uniform Transparency:** Applies an even transparency across the entire object.
- **Gradient Transparency:** Generates a gradual transition from opaque to transparent, which can be linear, radial, or customized.
- **Texture Transparency:** Utilizes patterns or textures to generate intricate transparency effects.

Advanced Transparency Techniques

1. **Interactive Transparency:** Real-time alterations are feasible through CorelDRAW's interactive transparency feature. The impact on your design is instantaneously apparent as you drag the transparency handle, which simplifies the process of fine-tuning its appearance.
2. **Transparency with Images:** Soft dissolves, overlays, or artistic effects can be achieved by applying transparency to images. For instance, by decreasing the opacity of a photograph, it is possible to achieve a seamless integration with a background or text.
3. **Combining Transparency with Effects:** To increase the visual complexity of your design, transparency can be combined with other effects, such as gradients, outlines, or shadows.

What Are Blending Modes?

How the colors of one object interact with the colors of the objects beneath it is regulated by blending modes. How the base color (the object below) and the composite color (the object on top) combine to produce the resulting color is determined by them.

Blending modes are especially useful for:
- Generating artistic effects.
- Enhancing a composition's atmosphere.
- Modifying the contrast, saturation, or luminosity of a design.

Common Blending Modes in CorelDRAW

CorelDRAW 2025 provides a diverse selection of blending modes, each with its distinctive features:
1. **Normal:** The default mode in which the upper object completely obscures the lower object, unless transparency is implemented.
2. **Multiply:** By compounding the base color with the composite color, the base color is darkened. This mode is advantageous for generating shadows or enhancing dimensionality.
3. **Screen:** By inverting and multiplying the base color with the composite color, the base color is lightened. Suitable for the production of gentle hues or highlights.
4. **Overlay:** Enhances contrast by integrating Screen and Multiply modes. This mode is ideal for enhancing the texture or dimension of an image by enhancing the contrast between light and dark areas.
5. **Soft Light:** Adds a subtle luminosity or darkness, contingent upon the color of the composite. It is frequently employed to generate mild illumination effects.
6. **Hard Light:** A more pronounced effect is achieved by combining Multiply and Screen. It is beneficial for the creation of high-contrast effects or dramatic illumination.
7. **Difference:** The base color is subtracted from the composite color, resulting in a high-contrast effect that highlights the distinctions between the two.
8. **Hue, Saturation, Color, and Luminosity:** These modes enable you to isolate and alter specific properties of the colors, such as modifying the hue or luminance exclusively.

How to Apply Blending Modes in CorelDRAW

1. Choose the object that you wish to blend.
2. Access the blending mode selection menu by opening the **Transparency Tool** or utilizing the **Property Bar**.
3. Select the desired blending mode. The specified mode's impact on the underlying objects will be instantaneously apparent in the updated result.
4. Adjust the transparency level or rearrange the layers to optimize the effect.

Using Transparency and Blending Modes Together

Sophisticated effects can be achieved by combining transparency and blending modes. For instance,
- A gentle shadow effect is generated by applying a **Multiply** blending mode to a semi-transparent object.
- The vibrancy of the underlying colors is preserved while the gradient is given depth by utilizing **Overlay** on a gradient transparency.

Intricate, visually captivating compositions can be generated by layering numerous objects with varying transparency levels and blending modes.

Practical Applications

1. **Photo Editing:** Utilize blending modes such as **Multiply** or **Screen** to modify the illumination, shadows, and highlights of images. Smooth transitions or vignettes can be achieved by incorporating gradient transparency.
2. **Text Effects:** Artistic typography can be achieved by combining text with merging modes and transparency. For example, the application of a Difference mode to text against a vibrant background results in a visually arresting, high-contrast effect.
3. **Backgrounds and Overlays:** Dynamic backgrounds can be generated by layering transparent objects with blending modes. For instance, a dreamlike, ethereal effect can be achieved by overlapping soft-light gradients.
4. **Branding and Loos:** Logos can be rendered more dynamic without overwhelming the design by incorporating subtle highlights, shadows, or gradients through transparency and blending modes.

Tips for Effective Use

1. **Experiment with Layers:** Arrange objects in layers and experiment with various transparency and blending modes to find the perfect balance.
2. **Preview on Different Backgrounds:** Transparency and blending modes can produce varying results depending on the background. It is imperative to test your design on both light and dark backgrounds to guarantee that it functions as intended.
3. **Optimize for Printing:** If your design is intended for print, exercise caution when utilizing transparency and blending modes, as certain printers may encounter difficulties with these effects. To prevent unexpected outcomes, flatten transparency before exporting.
4. **Use Subtlety:** An overuse of blending modes or transparency can result in a design that appears congested. Utilize these tools with caution to improve your composition, rather than to overwhelm it.

Drop Shadows and Glow

Creating a Drop Shadow

1. **Choose the object**: To begin, choose the object that you wish to enhance with a shadow. This may manifest as an image, text, or shape. Ensure that the object is the active selection by using the **Pick Tool** to click on it.
2. **Activate the Drop Shadow Tool:** Select the **Drop Shadow Tool** by navigating to the **Toolbox** on the left side of your workspace. If it is not immediately visible, click and hold the tool group to expand the list, as it can be grouped with other interactive tools.
3. **Apply the Shadow:** Click on the object and drag your cursor outward in the direction in which you wish the shadow to materialize while the **Drop Shadow Tool** is active. A preview of the shadow emanating from the object will be displayed as you drag. When the shadow has reached the desired extent, release the mouse trigger.

4. **Refine the Shadow:** The shadow's properties can be further refined by utilizing the **Property Bar** located at the top of the workspace after it has been applied. In this section, you can modify:
    - **Opacity:** Adjust the opacity percentage to determine the transparency or solidity of the shadow.
    - **Feathering:** Modify the feathering value to alter the delicacy of the shadow's boundaries. A more diffuse, natural-looking shadow is the consequence of increased feathering.
    - **Angle and Distance:** Adjust the angle and distance values to alter the direction and offset of the shadow with the object.
    - **Color:** Adjust the shadow color as necessary. Although black is the default, shadows that are paler or colored can create unique effects?
5. **Reposition the Shadow:** To relocate the shadow, utilize the **Drop Shadow Tool** to click and drag it to a new location. This is particularly beneficial for ensuring that the shadow is in alignment with a particular light source in your composition.
6. **Finalize and Apply:** Select the object by selecting anywhere outside the workspace once you are satisfied with the shadow. The drop shadow has been incorporated into your design; however, it is still modifiable if you require modifications at a later time.

Creating a Glow Effect

1. **Choose the Object:** Select the object to which you wish to apply the glow effect. This can be a shape, text, or image, similar to the shadow.
2. **Convert to Bitmap (if necessary):** Glows in CorelDRAW are frequently most effective when applied to bitmap objects. To achieve a gentle, diffused radiance on a vector object, convert it to a bitmap by selecting **Bitmaps > Convert to Bitmap**. If necessary, ensure that the background is transparent and select a resolution of at least 300 DPI to achieve high-quality results.
3. **Apply the Glow Effect:** Navigate to the Effects menu located at the top of the workspace and select **Creative > Glow**. This initiates the Glow dialog box, which allows you to personalize the effect.
4. **Adjust Glow Properties:** The Glow dialog box contains a variety of settings that can be adjusted to optimize the effect:
    - **Glow Color:** Select the desired color for the luminescence. Vibrant effects are frequently achieved through the use of bright or complementary colors.
    - **Glow Intensity:** Regulate the intensity of the light, ranging from subtle to intense. For a dramatic, startling effect, increase the intensity, or decrease it for a softer, more natural appearance.
    - **Glow Size:** Modify the glow's magnitude to ascertain its distance from the object. An aura-like effect is produced by larger flames, while a focused outline is provided by tiny ones.
    - **Transparency:** Adjust the transparency level of the light to ensure that it blends seamlessly with the background.
5. **Preview the Glow:** A live preview displays the appearance of the luminescence on your object as you modify the settings. Use the sliders to experiment until you attain the desired appearance.
6. **Apply the Effect:** The glow effect will be applied by clicking **OK** once you are satisfied with the glow settings. Your object's visual prominence is now enhanced by the radiance that is now visible around it.
7. **Additional Refinements:** If additional modifications are required, you can return to the Glow dialog box or employ the **Transparency Tool** to alter the glow's intensity and merge with the background.

Combining Drop Shadows and Glows

To generate more dynamic and multilayered effects, it is possible to combine drop shadows and lights. For instance,

- Apply a subtle tint to the text and then add a drop shadow to make it stand out against a busy background.
- Incorporate a complementary radiance and a colored shadow to enhance the vibrancy and depth of objects in abstract designs.

It is crucial to avoid the design being overpowered when combining effects. Maintain equilibrium by adjusting the opacity and magnitude of each effect.

Tips for Using Drop Shadows and Glows Effectively

- **Keep it Realistic:** When employing shadows, take into account the light source in your composition. To preserve a genuine appearance, shadows must be consistent in both direction and intensity.
- **Use Subtlety for Professional Designs:** A design that is overly reliant on strong shadows or hues may appear unsophisticated. Effects that are well-integrated and subtle are frequently more effective for the majority of projects.
- **Experiment with Colors:** Although black shadows and white glows are conventional, incorporating colored shadows or glows can provide a distinctive element to your design.
- **Test on Different Backgrounds:** Ensure that your shadows and hues appear visually appealing on a variety of backgrounds, particularly if your design will be utilized in diverse contexts.

Inserting 3D Effects in Objects in CorelDraw

Bevel Effects Creation

By generating the appearance of sloped edges, bevel effects add a sense of three-dimensional depth to the text or graphic object. The bevel effects can be suitable for printing, as they may encompass both process (CMYK) and spot hues.

Bevel Styles

We have the option to choose from the following bevel styles:

- o **Soft Edge:** It is used to create beveled surfaces that appear shaded in certain areas.
- o **Emboss:** This process generates an object that resembles a relief.

To achieve the smooth edge effect

1. Select any object that is capable of being closed and contains the fill that was applied to it.

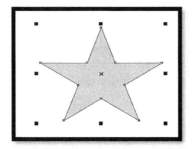

2. Select "**Effects**" and then "**Bevel**."

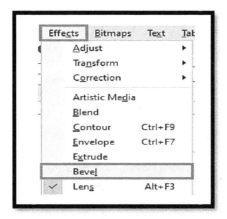

3. Select "**Soft edge**" from the "**Style**" list box in the Bevel docker.
4. Allow any individual to adjust the **Bevel offset**:
    ○   **To Center:** This allows for the creation of beveled surfaces that intersect in the object's center.
    ○   **Distance:** It allows us to specify the breadth of the beveled surface. Enter the value in the **Distance**.

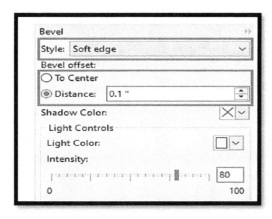

Extrusion Creation

Extrusion is a method that can be employed to generate a three-dimensional appearance for objects. We can generate an extrusion by projecting points through any object and subsequently joining them to create a 3D illusion. CorelDRAW allows us to apply vector extrusion to the object within the group.

- o Utilizing the beveled edge of an extrusion is another method by which we can give the object a 3D appearance.
- o Fills can be employed to cover the entire extrusion or a specific extruded surface.
- o Light sources can be employed to enhance extrusion.
- o Additionally, we can furnish the extrusions with unique vanishing points.

Make the extrusion

1. Select the object using the **Pick**.
2. Press the **Extrude** button located in the toolbar.

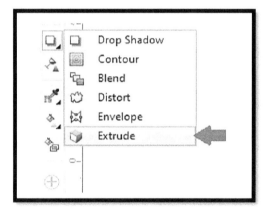

3. Through the **Presets** list box located above the property bar, choose the desired preset.

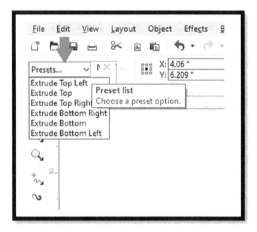

4. In the **Extrusion type** list box located above the Property Bar, select the desired extrusion type.

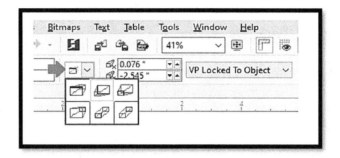

To reset an extrusion, click **Esc** before releasing the mouse cursor. The **Extrude** docker **(Effects > Extrude)** can also be used to perform the extrusion.

Perspective Usage to Objects

The perspective effects can be achieved by shortening one or two sides of the object. It creates a two-point or one-point perspective by illustrating the objects' receding in two or one direction. Various objects could be incorporated with perspective effects. Additionally, these effects can be incorporated into numerous linked groups, including **extrusion**, **blends**, and **contour**. Symbols, bitmaps, and paragraph text are not eligible for perspective effects. These effects can be applied to other objects within a drawing, or they can be removed or adjusted through the object.

Employ the perspective

o Click on **Effects** and select "**Add perspective**."

To achieve any desired effect, relocate the nodes to the exterior of the grid. **Note:** The perspective effect can be replicated by utilizing the Attribute eyedropper tool.

Contouring Objects

We can contour any object to create a series of concentric lines that progress at either the object's exterior or interior. The distance and number of contour lines can be configured in CorelDRAW. To generate output on certain devices, such as vinyl cutters, engraving machines, and plotters, contours can be implemented to generate cuttable outlines.

Contour the object

1. Press the **Contour** tool located in the toolbar.

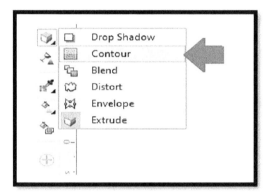

2. Press the set of any grouped object or any object and move the aperture handle to the center to create the inside contour or from the center to create the outside contour.

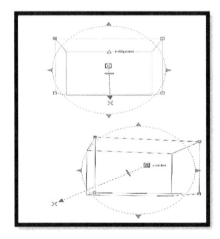

3. The number of contour steps can be adjusted by dragging an object slider.

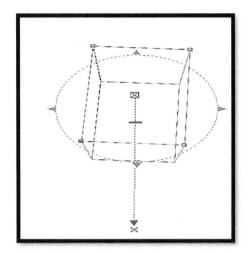

Using CorelDRAW's Perspective Tool for Dynamic Designs

The ability to generate dynamic designs in CorelDRAW can be a game-changing experience for any designer. The Perspective Tool in CorelDRAW enables users to convert ordinary designs into breathtaking, three-dimensional visuals. **By mastering this tool, designers can effortlessly incorporate depth and dimension into their artwork, thereby enhancing its realism and appeal.** It is essential to comprehend the proper utilization of the Perspective Tool. It provides designers with the ability to present their conceptions in a variety of ways, including two-point and three-point perspectives. This tool has the potential to enhance the professionalism and creativity of a design by demonstrating its potential in real-world applications. To initiate its utilization, designers may modify field density and drag nodes to implement a two-point perspective.

Core Concepts of Perspective Drawing

Constructing the illusion of three-dimensional space on a two-dimensional surface is the art technique of perspective drawing. It consists of lines that terminate at a point on the horizon, which is referred to as the vanishing point. The profundity of their designs can be enhanced by allowing artists to select from one-point, two-point, or three-point perspectives in CorelDRAW. One-point perspective is most suitable for objects that are directly in front of the observer and have a single vanishing point. Corner views of objects are facilitated by a two-point perspective, which features two vanishing points. A third vanishing point is introduced in a three-point perspective to provide an overhead or ground-level perspective. Users can effortlessly transition between these perspectives and modify the perspective field with CorelDRAW's Perspective Tool. This adaptability facilitates the development of dynamic designs that interactively simulate real-world perspectives.

Locating the Perspective Tool in CorelDRAW

CorelDRAW's Perspective Tool is located in the Object menu. Before accessing the utility, users should guarantee that no objects are selected. Click on **Object**, then navigate to **Perspective** and select **Draw in Perspective.** The tool provides a type list box in which users can select various perspectives after selecting them. The perspective field is then established by the user through click-and-drag actions in the drawing window, which enables them to exert precise control over the depth and dimension of their designs. This user-friendly configuration facilitates the process of generating perspective views, rendering it accessible to individuals who are new to digital art. The tool is intended to foster creativity while simultaneously preserving a simple and intuitive approach.

Setting Up Your Workspace for Perspective Designs

It is crucial to establish a workspace that is customized to your design requirements to begin utilizing CorelDRAW's perspective tool. This entails the development of a new document that is optimized for perspective drawing and the customization of the interface to accommodate individual preferences.

Customizing the Interface

A versatile interface is provided by CorelDRAW to optimize workflow efficacy. Users should commence by modifying the toolbar to ensure that it contains perspective drawing tools. This arrangement expedites the design process. Dockers, which are tiny panels that offer options related to specific tools, can also be customized. Users can effortlessly access perspective options by incorporating pertinent dockers. Another step in the process of streamlining actions is the customization of shortcuts. To minimize the time spent navigating menus, assign keys to frequently used tools. The final step is to ensure that the design work is consistent by selecting the appropriate color palette. Users can generate personalized palettes that include colors that are frequently employed. This can result in more cohesive perspective drawings.

Creating a New Document for Perspective Work

It is imperative to establish a separate document that is dedicated to perspective illustrations. Open CorelDRAW and select a blank canvas. Users can modify the dimensions and settings to suit the specific requirements of the project. It is essential to select the appropriate units for perspective work. Select from a variety of units, including millimeters, centimeters, or other units that align with the design specifications. Establish dimensions that are appropriate for the specific undertaking after determining the units. Next, navigate to the **Object** menu and select **Perspective > Draw in Perspective.** This action activates CorelDRAW's perspective grid, which is customizable following the design's complexity. Incorporating a perspective field facilitates the alignment of components within the perspective framework. This framework functions as a framework for designs that are well-aligned and dynamic.

Creating Basic Shapes with Perspective

The perspective tool in CorelDRAW simplifies the process of incorporating depth and dimension into common shapes, such as ellipses, circles, squares, and rectangles. Users can generate designs that are more dynamic by modifying these shapes.

Drawing Rectangles and Squares

Users must initially activate the perspective mode in CorelDRAW to create rectangles and squares with perspective. This can be accomplished by selecting **Object > Perspective > Draw in Perspective**. Upon activation, a perspective grid is displayed. Users can employ the **Rectangle tool** to create the desired shape within this grid. The three-dimensional appearance of the shape will be achieved by adhering to the perspective lines. Further customization is facilitated by adjusting the nodes at the corners. Users can manipulate the vanishing points to enhance the realism. How the rectangle or square appears to taper off into the distance is regulated by these. This element is essential for achieving a realistic depth and ensuring that the design is consistent with other components.

Manipulating Circles and Ellipses

A slightly different approach is necessary to create circles and ellipses in perspective. To initiate the perspective grid, select **Object > Perspective > Draw in Perspective**. The **Ellipse tool** can be employed to create a circle or ellipse once the perspective mode has been established. The perspective grid assists in the transformation of these shapes into ovals or elongated circles that appear to recede into space. The shape's aspect can be further altered by adjusting the nodes. Users can expand or compress the circles and ellipses by clicking and dragging. This adaptability enables the structures to be seamlessly integrated into any design.

Advanced Techniques

The perspective tool in CorelDRAW can substantially improve designs through the application of sophisticated techniques. Using these methods, users can distort text within a perspective grid to add depth to objects and create a dynamic feeling.

Adding Depth to Objects

To achieve depth in objects using CorelDRAW, it is necessary to manipulate perspectives to emphasize certain elements. Designers can simulate three-dimensional effects by employing the **Object Perspective** feature. This utility enables users to modify angles and perspective lines, thereby facilitating the creation of realistic drawings. Begin by selecting an object and implementing the perspective grid. Subsequently, manipulate the anchor points of the grid to modify the object's apparent depth and angle. To increase the level of complexity, the composition can be enhanced by incorporating objects from various perspectives, which results in a more realistic appearance. Designers can enhance their illustrations by offering a more immersive and engaging visual experience through the implementation of these methods. The illusion of depth is further enhanced by the addition of shadows and highlights, which create the illusion that objects are emerging from the screen.

Distorting Text for Perspective

Designs are rendered more dynamic by distorting text in perspective. By utilizing CorelDRAW's text tools, users can adjust letters to ensure that they are in alignment with perspective grids, thereby generating an engaging graphical element. Initially, implement perspective distortion by converting text to curves. This conversion enables the editing of text paths like that of vector shapes. Then, select the perspective tool, drag the text to align with the desired perspective, and modify it to its desired position. To preserve legibility, the text must be aligned with the grid. Furthermore, experiment with the use of colors and shading to enhance the style and substance of your text. This technique is particularly effective for headings or any design element that requires prominence within a composition.

Manipulating and Adjusting Perspective Views

Designers can generate dynamic and captivating visuals by employing CorelDRAW's perspective tool. To optimize the visual impact, the perspective angle is adjusted and the depth of field is refined.

Changing the Perspective Angle

The adjustment of the perspective angle is essential for the creation of dynamic scenes. The tool provided by CorelDRAW enables users to effortlessly select the perspective they desire, including 1-point, 2-point, and 3-point. How observers perceive depth and distance is influenced by this decision. Use the controls that appear around the perspective grid to adjust the angle. Swivel or tilt the grid by dragging these controls to ensure that it is following the requirements of your design. This adaptability enables designers to create illustrations that are more realistic or stylized as needed for their projects, thereby accommodating unique perspectives. A planar design can be transformed into a three-dimensional visual masterpiece by altering the perspective angle. Designers particularly appreciate this feature when they are endeavoring to illustrate intricate scenes or architecture with greater dimensions.

Fine-Tuning the Depth of Field

By adjusting the depth of field, designers can regulate the perceived profundity of the scene. The visual space can be either expanded or contracted by manipulating nodes within the perspective grid. This assists in emphasizing specific components of a design while simultaneously obscuring others. CorelDRAW provides precise control over depth adjustments. Designers should prioritize the preservation of accurate scaling to prevent the appearance of distorted objects. When coping with sophisticated layouts or multiple objects, this feature is essential. The depth of field can be adjusted to improve the narrative in visuals. It ensures that the primary message is prominently displayed while maintaining the harmony of the entire composition by directing the viewer's attention to the most critical components of the design.

Creative Applications of the Perspective Tool

The CorelDRAW Perspective Tool can transform basic designs into dynamic works of art. It is particularly beneficial for the development of visually appealing logos and the enhancement of the profundity of intricate scenes. This tool imparts a sense of sophistication and realism to designs.

Designing Logos with Perspective

The perspective tool can be used to create logos that are more visually appealing and distinctive. A flat logo can be given depth and dimension by incorporating perspective. This approach can be employed to display the brand's name in a flamboyant and innovative manner. The perspective tool enables designers to adjust or angle text and objects. This may necessitate a two-point perspective, in which the logo extends toward two distinct vanishing points. The logo is perceived as more three-dimensional by incorporating perspective. This method is ideal for brands that desire a contemporary and distinctive appearance. Elements are given a distinctive perspective through meticulous adjustments, which improves the overall visual appeal.

Crafting Complex Scenes

Another thrilling application of the perspective tool is the creation of complex scenes. It enables artists to construct environments that are both realistic and deep, thereby enhancing the design's richness. Designers can create scenes in which objects organically recede into the distance by employing a variety of perspective types, such as one-point or three-point. This is particularly advantageous when depicting structures, streets, or other intricate scenes. Designers are capable of rapidly manipulating and aligning elements to accommodate the desired perspective. This allows them to create vibrant and realistic pieces by illustrating locations such as cityscapes or landscapes. It is a potent tool for the creation of dynamic and immersive compositions.

Using the Envelope Tool

The Envelope Tool in CorelDRAW is a potent tool for manipulating text and objects. It facilitates the development of dynamic and visually appealing designs by altering the shape and form of text.

Defining the Envelope Tool

The Envelope Tool enables users to reshape or distort objects. It is a component of the Effects tool category in CorelDRAW. This utility enables the creation of distinctive effects by stretching, compressing, or skewing various components of a text or object. This is especially beneficial for the development of logos, advertisements, or any other graphic design project that necessitates a personal touch. Designers have the option of selecting from pre-existing envelope shapes or generating their own, rendering it a versatile tool. Additionally, the utility offers the ability to manually modify nodes, which allows for more precise control over the distortion effect. This tool enables designers to generate professional-looking graphics without the need for supplementary software.

Accessing the Envelope Tool in CorelDRAW

Begin by selecting the object or text that you desire to modify in CorelDRAW to utilize the Envelope Tool. To access it on a PC, navigate to **Window > Dockers > Effects > Envelope** or enter **Ctrl + F7.** The shortcut for Mac users is **Shift + Ctrl + E.** The property bar will display options and functions related to the envelope effect once the utility is opened. Afterward, users have the option to implement these settings to their objects by either customizing the nodes or utilizing the predefined structures. Users can rapidly and efficiently enhance their creative endeavors by conquering these steps and controls. The tool's intuitive interface is user-friendly, enabling even novices to effortlessly investigate a wide range of design options.

Preparing Your Text for Distortion

It is crucial to appropriately configure text boxes and select the appropriate font before employing CorelDRAW's Envelope Tool for creative effects. These procedures guarantee that the final product is both professional and refined.

Selecting the Appropriate Font

It is essential to select the appropriate font when composing text for distortion. The most effective typefaces are frequently simple and forceful, as they maintain readability even when they are warped. Sans-serif fonts, such as Helvetica or Arial, are frequently employed. These fonts are devoid of decorative elements that can cause them to become unrecognizable. It is possible that serif fonts with intricate details can lose their clarity. Font size is also a factor. It is generally preferable to use larger text, as tiny letters can become difficult to comprehend when they are altered. It is essential to experiment with various fonts and sizes to determine the most effective approach for achieving the desired outcome.

Creating Text Boxes for Envelope Application

After selecting the font, it is time to establish text areas in CorelDRAW. Initially, either create a new document or select an existing one. Then, employ the Text Tool to generate text boxes. To preserve the design's balance, it is advantageous to align these frames appropriately. Text frames should be designed to accommodate the content in a tight fit, with minimal space remaining around the text. During distortion, this configuration mitigates unforeseen changes. If additional manipulation is required, guarantee that the text is converted to curves. This method preserves the design and opens up additional inventive opportunities when the Envelope Tool is employed.

Basic Operations of the Envelope Tool

By applying or modifying envelopes to shapes, the Envelope Tool in CorelDRAW enables users to generate distinctive text effects. This section delineates the process of manually adjusting envelope nodes for custom designs and utilizing preset envelopes.

Applying a Preset Envelope

Begin by selecting the text or shape that you wish to modify in the preset envelopes. The Envelope Tool is a component of the Effects category. To access the Envelope docker on Windows, type **Ctrl + F7**. For Mac users, enter the following keys: **Shift + Ctrl + E.** The Envelope docker's options facilitate the selection of a preset once it is opened. These configurations consist of single-arc, double-arc, and straight-line designs. Click on the design you have selected, and it will be immediately applied to the object you have selected. Presets are perfect for quick adjustments and adding flair without detailed manual changes. They are also a great way to get a consistent look across similar elements. Remember, these envelope styles maintain the design integrity while giving you creative control over text and shape appearances.

Adjusting the Envelope Nodes Manually

Create custom shapes by manually adjusting the envelope nodes for greater control. To begin, choose the object that requires modification. Subsequently, activate the **Envelope Tool** to generate nodes on the object's boundaries. To modify the position of any node, simply click on it. By double-clicking along the boundary where you desire additional control, you can add new nodes or eliminate them by double-clicking on a node that is no longer required. By relocating these nodes, it is possible to generate complex curves and bends. The design is distinctive due to the precise customization that manual alterations enable. Although it necessitates an additional amount of time, the creative autonomy is well worth the effort. Artists are empowered to create designs that are genuinely consistent with their vision by manually adjusting nodes.

Customizing Text Distortions

The Envelope Tool is employed to refine the appearance of distorted text in CorelDRAW. This encompasses the addition of new nodes to generate distinctive shapes and the manipulation of segments to achieve precise results. Both methods assist in attaining the precise appearance that is desired.

Adding New Envelope Nodes

Users can generate more intricate shapes and text distortions by incorporating nodes into the envelope. To accomplish this, select the **Envelope Tool** and click on the text you wish to modify. By tapping on the path, users can subsequently add nodes along the envelope outline. Each node permits modifications, including the relocation or curvature of the line to accommodate particular design requirements. The addition of new nodes increases the adaptability of shapes, which in turn facilitates the creation of complex designs. The uniformity and flow of the distortions are influenced by the number and positioning of nodes. Incremental adjustments are recommended due to the importance of precision. This approach is optimal for custom shapes and effects that necessitate meticulous customization.

Manipulating Envelope Segments

Text distortion can be further controlled by manipulating the segments between nodes. In CorelDRAW, segments can be modified by dragging and selecting them or by utilizing control points for curves. This enables users to adjust the angle and flow of text or shapes. The capacity to modify segments is indispensable for optimizing the envelope's visual appeal. By reshaping curves and leveling out angles, designers can generate seamless twists and turns. This method is especially beneficial for the development of designs that are both fluid and well-balanced. Experimenting with the length and direction of segments can result in unexpected and artistic text effects. It fosters creativity by providing a variety of design options, ensuring that each endeavor is unique.

Advanced Distortion Techniques

Users can manipulate text into distinctive shapes and forms by employing advanced distortion techniques in CorelDRAW's Envelope Tool. These methods can be employed to produce visually arresting effects and to improve the artistic allure of text in graphic designs.

Creating Irregular Shape Distortions

Text can be rendered more dynamic and captivating by incorporating irregular shape distortions. Users can use the interactive capabilities of CorelDRAW's Envelope Tool to accomplish this. The distortion can be customized to meet the specific design requirements by adjusting the control handles and nodes. This method is particularly advantageous for the development of headlines or logos that require prominence. Designers can extend, contract, or bend text by manipulating the shape's nodes. The tool's adaptability enables users to generate organic and asymmetrical shapes, which enhances the personalization of any design project.

Applying Effects to Distorted Text

The visual impact can be further enhanced by applying a variety of effects after the text has been distorted. Shadows and gradients can emphasize the distorted shape, rendering it more three-dimensional. In CorelDRAW, users can fine-tune settings to accomplish the desired appearance by utilizing the tool property bar. When utilizing effects on distorted text, creativity is essential. Designers can accomplish a diverse range of designs, from vintage and artistic to sleek and modern, by experimenting with various colors and textures. These methods guarantee that the text is not only distinct and visually appealing, but also functional.

Best Practices for Envelope Tool Use

Maintaining legibility is essential when employing CorelDRAW's Envelope Tool to apply distortions. This tool can also improve logo design by enabling the use of distinctive shapes and effects that are consistent with the brand's identity.

Maintaining Readability with Distortions

The Envelope Tool can generate captivating visual effects by distorting text; however, it is crucial to ensure that the text remains intelligible. Begin by selecting the appropriate font, as simplified fonts are frequently the most effective when distorted. They guarantee that critical letters are identifiable even after they transform. Utilize the preview feature of the Envelope Tool regularly. This enables the distortion to be adjusted as necessary before the finalization. Refrain from employing extreme distortions that enlarge text excessively, as they may impede comprehension. Frequently, a more professional and streamlined appearance can be achieved by making minor adjustments to the tool. Play around with the various configurations that are accessible in the Envelope Tool. These presets offer a diverse selection of shapes and can serve as an effective starting point. Ensure that the final output is clear by inspecting it from various distances or sizes.

Utilizing Envelope Tool for Logo Design

The Envelope Tool is an excellent tool for the development of dynamic logos. It enables designers to customize the text and graphics to more effectively convey the brand's message. Begin by integrating shapes that are indicative of the organization's identity. To accommodate intricate designs, stack numerous envelopes. This method has the potential to enhance the profundity and interest of logos, thereby enhancing their visibility. Place a high value on proportion and symmetry to ensure that the design is aesthetically appealing and cohesive. Rotate and scale envelope shapes with precision. This versatility enables logos to be both distinguishing and authentic to the brand. Lastly, verify the logo's appearance on a variety of backgrounds and sizes to guarantee that it remains effective across a variety of media.

Troubleshooting Common Issues

Users may experience issues such as text overlap and unwanted distortion effects when employing CorelDRAW's Envelope Tool. Clean and professional outcomes are guaranteed by addressing these obstacles.

Handling Text Overlap Problems

Text overlap can occur when enclosures are adjusted, particularly when the shapes are more intricate or constrictive. Users can begin by selecting the text and modifying the node positions on the envelope path to resolve this issue. This can involve moving or deleting nodes to reduce crowding. An additional approach is to modify the node identifiers. Users can reshape the envelope path to increase the space between letters or words by dragging these handles. The "**Fit Text to Path**" option can also assist in the seamless alignment and adjustment of text around curves. If it is necessary, the text can be divided into smaller segments to facilitate more precise control. Additionally, it is advantageous to focus in closely analyze how each letter is accommodated within the envelope. The identification of problem areas that require adjustment is facilitated by a thorough examination. Users can reduce the tension associated with the process by frequently saving and reverting to previous versions if necessary.

Correcting Distortion Artefacts

Text can appear unequal or distended in an undesirable manner as a result of distortion artifacts. The envelope intensity can be reduced by users to begin addressing this issue. A more natural appearance is achieved by reducing the effect. An additional approach that proves advantageous is to implement minute modifications to the envelope curve. Users can eliminate any undesirable distortions by adjusting the curvature and relocating control points. It may be necessary to experiment with various envelope modes if the text continues to appear erroneous. Testing alternatives such as single arc or double arcs could be effective, as certain modes have a greater impact on distortion than others. To achieve the best possible outcome, it is essential to strike a balance between readability and artistic impact. Users can maintain their focus by conducting frequent inspections of the text and implementing incremental modifications. One final suggestion is that users should frequently compare each modification to the original text to guarantee that the design remains following their intentions.

CHAPTER EIGHT

WORKING WITH LAYERS

Understanding Layers in CorelDRAW

In CorelDRAW, layers enable designers to organize elements according to their significance or function. CorelDRAW generates a default layer, frequently referred to as **Layer 1**, upon commencing a new project. This layer can be renamed, and additional layers can be incorporated as required. Users can activate a layer by selecting its name in the Object Manager, which is highlighted in red to signify activity. Layers can be concealed or secured to prevent unintended modifications. **Master layers** are unique in that they extend across all pages, making them particularly beneficial for elements such as headings. Organization is substantially enhanced by the establishment of distinct layers for backgrounds, images, and text. Designers can work on numerous areas without any cluttered spaces as a result of this structured approach.

Benefits of Using Layers

Improved control over various design elements is a significant advantage of employing layers. The risk of influencing other components of the design is reduced by the ability to make modifications independently with layers. This method is especially advantageous for projects that necessitate precision. Additionally, layers facilitate more efficient productivity, enabling users to effortlessly navigate intricate designs. Designers can concentrate on specific elements, such as colors or text, without being interrupted. Furthermore, layers are beneficial for repetitive advertising duties, as they ensure that the project maintains consistent designs. The utilization of strata also facilitates collaboration. Multiple designers can work on distinct sections simultaneously without disrupting each other's work. This makes layers a valuable aid for both novice and experienced users, as it reduces errors and enhances productivity.

Getting Started with Layers

The ability to utilize layers in CorelDRAW can significantly alter the process of creating and editing graphics. The efficient organization and management of intricate designs are contingent upon the mastery of the initial steps.

Opening the Layers Panel

Locating the Layers panel, which is referred to as the Objects docker on Windows or the Objects inspector on Mac, is the initial stage in working with layers in CorelDRAW. This is the location where users can observe, create, and organize layers. To access this interface on Windows, select **Window > Dockers > Objects**. For Mac users, the process is as follows: **Window > Inspectors > Objects**. It is essential to open the panel, as it enables the construction of new layers and displays existing ones. Establishing the foundation for effective graphic design is facilitated by comprehending this layout.

Creating Your First Layer

The subsequent action is to generate your initial layer after the Layers interface has been opened. CorelDRAW typically initiates a new document with a default layer named **Layer 1**. To incorporate a layer, merely select the **New Layer** icon located in the interface. This new layer can be named and customized to meet the specific requirements of the user. Layers are a method for organizing various elements of a design, including text, images, and shapes. Additionally, the utilization of layers can facilitate the management of design elements discretely, thereby simplifying the process of editing without influencing the entire artwork. This method not only increases the flexibility of design initiatives but also saves time. Users can concentrate on a single aspect at a time, which guarantees the completion of detailed and precise work.

Layer Management

In CorelDRAW, layer management entails the renaming, duplication, and deletion of layers. These responsibilities facilitate the organization and efficiency of your design process, thereby simplifying the process of producing intricate illustrations.

Renaming Layers

Organization is simplified by renaming layers in CorelDRAW. It facilitates the rapid identification of the purpose of each layer by users. Initially, the **Object Manager** must be accessed to rename a layer. To activate the layer, simply click on its name. When the layer is selected, its name is displayed in a prominent, red font. Right-clicking on the layer name displays the option to rename it. Selecting a descriptive moniker is beneficial for recalling the contents of each stratum. It is crucial to maintain a concise yet comprehensive name. It improves the workflow, particularly during intricate projects.

Duplicating Layers

Users can utilize elements in their designs by duplicating layers. Using the **Object Manager** in CorelDRAW, this procedure can be executed. The layer that users wish to duplicate should be selected. After selecting the layer, right-click on it and select the **duplicate** option. All properties of the original layer are inherited by duplicated layers, which results in a reduction in time. When designing similar designs or reiterating patterns across multiple layers, this function proves advantageous. Duplicating is also beneficial for conducting experiments that do not involve modifying the original layer. This fosters exploration and creativity in design projects.

Deleting Layers

It is imperative to eliminate layers to eliminate superfluous components. The Objects docker in CorelDRAW enables the deletion of layers. Initially, the appropriate stratum must be activated. To delete, select the **delete** option by right-clicking on the name of the active layer. Users should exercise caution when deleting, as this action is not always reversible. The content of the layer is verified before deletion to prevent the inadvertent loss of critical design elements. The maintenance of a spotless and efficient workspace is facilitated by the proper management of layer deletion. This guarantees that only pertinent layers are included, which facilitates a more efficient design process.

Organizing Artwork with Layers

Using layers in CorelDRAW is beneficial for maintaining the organization and manageability of any artwork. Users can improve the efficiency and precision of their designs by arranging layers, modifying their stacking order, organizing layers logically, and controlling their visibility.

Sorting and Stacking Order

To effectively manage intricate designs, it is essential to sort and arrange layers in CorelDRAW. In the Layers interface, layers can be rearranged by dragging and moving them. This aids in the regulation of which elements are displayed above or below others. An upper layer is discernible above the layers beneath it. When working with numerous elements, it is crucial to sort them to enable designers to concentrate on specific components without interference. The design process is expedited and access is facilitated by positioning frequently used elements at the top. The artwork's visual hierarchy is crucial for clarity, and effective layering ensures that it is maintained.

Grouping Layers

In CorelDRAW, layer grouping is an efficient method for organizing related elements. Designers can combine multiple layers by utilizing the **Group** function. This simplifies the process of applying effects, resizing, or moving all elements simultaneously. Grouping is beneficial for maintaining consistency when dealing with repetitive elements. It is particularly advantageous for guaranteeing consistency throughout various components of the design. Furthermore, layers that are grouped can be rapidly degrouped for individual modification, thereby enabling greater flexibility. Grouping streamlines the workspace, reducing its congestion and facilitating its navigation. It is an invaluable tool for the management of complex designs with numerous components, enabling the execution of more efficient and expedited modification processes.

Layer Visibility

CorelDRAW's layer visibility feature enables designers to conceal or reveal layers as required. This is accomplished by selecting the eye icon located adjacent to the layer in the Layers interface. By concealing layers, the view can be simplified, allowing for a more concentrated focus on specific areas without any distractions. When working on comprehensive projects or printing specific elements, it is especially beneficial to adjust layer visibility. Designers can more effectively focus on the task at hand by momentarily concealing layers. This function facilitates the simulation of the interaction between various elements without permanently affecting the design. CorelDRAW is a versatile tool for designers, as it is essential for preserving workflow efficiency, ensuring greater control, and reducing errors in complex artwork by managing visibility.

Working with Layer Properties

Users can more effectively manage and refine their designs by comprehending the properties of layers in CorelDRAW. This entails the customization of layer colors to facilitate simple identification and the management of layer-locking mechanisms to prevent inadvertent modifications.

Locking Layers

The ability to lock layers is a critical component of maintaining the integrity of your design. Locking a layer prevents it from being moved or modified, which is especially advantageous when working on intricate projects with numerous components. This function serves to prevent unintentional modifications or modifications that could potentially undermine the design. To secure a layer, the user must access the **Object Manager** and select the lock icon located next to the layer name. This straightforward procedure guarantees that the layer is not influenced by any modifications made to other layers in the project. Especially when working with intricate designs that contain overlapping elements, designing with protected layers can reduce errors and save time. This function is especially advantageous when working with others, as it safeguards specific components of a project.

Changing Layer Color

In CorelDRAW, altering the color of a layer is a practical method for organizing and distinguishing between different components of your design. Users can promptly identify and manipulate specific components of a project by assigning a unique color to each layer. This visual organization has the potential to simplify the administration of intricate designs. To modify the color of a layer, select the layer in the **Object Manager** and click on its color swatch. The outline color of objects on that layer can be updated by selecting a new color from the palette. This customization improves visibility, enabling the rapid identification of active or inert layers. It is a practical approach for designers who frequently transition between layers and require a clear understanding of their document structure.

Advanced Layer Functions

Users can more effectively manage intricate projects by acquiring knowledge of sophisticated layer functions in CorelDRAW. These functions encompass the creation of layer groups, the coupling of layers, and the merging of layers. Each offers distinctive advantages for organizing complex designs.

Creating Layer Groups

Users can simultaneously manage multiple layers by establishing layer groups in CorelDRAW. Designers can save time and effort by applying transformations, such as scaling or rotating, to the entire group by grouping layers. To establish a layer group, select the desired layers in the Objects docker and employ the grouping function. This is particularly beneficial when managing substantial design files, as it facilitates the maintenance of an organized workspace. Layer grouping is particularly advantageous for components that require coordination, thereby enhancing the efficacy and uniformity of design projects.

Linking Layers

The act of linking layers in CorelDRAW facilitates the preservation of a connection between various layers. For projects that necessitate consistent modifications across multiple elements, this feature is indispensable. Changes made to one layer are automatically applied to the others when layers are linked, thereby guaranteeing uniformity. Users must activate the linking option and select the corresponding layers in the Objects docker to connect them. This feature is advantageous for the preservation of a consistent design aesthetic. It guarantees that related elements remain consistent and organized, thereby simplifying the design process and enabling more straightforward updates.

Merging Layers

The ability to merge layers is essential for the completion of designs and the reduction of file complexity. It enhances the design's manageability and minimizes the probability of errors or inadvertent alterations by consolidating selected layers into a single entity. To merge layers, select the layers you wish to combine in the Objects docker and select the **Merge** option. This action leads to a more efficient file, as there are fewer layers to navigate. After all modifications have been made, merging is particularly beneficial for simplifying designs, optimizing the file for printing or exporting, and creating a cleaner workspace.

Layer Effects and Styles

Your work in CorelDRAW can be substantially improved by layer effects and designs. They provide inventive opportunities to modify visual elements by reusing stored styles and applying a variety of effects to ensure consistency across projects.

Applying Effects to Layers

Layer effects in CorelDRAW offer a plethora of creative opportunities. The appearance of individual layers can be modified without affecting the original content by adjusting the effects. To improve visual dimensionality, users can implement effects such as reflections, flames, or shadows. To implement effects, select a layer and utilize the **Layer Styles** icon. This initiates the Layer Properties dialog window. Users are presented with a selection of effects, including Shadow and Reflection. The settings of each effect are adjustable, enabling the precise customization of the desired outcome. This adaptability allows artists to generate distinctive visuals that are distinctive.

Saving and Re-using Layer Styles

Saving an effective design can simplify future endeavors. Users can preserve a consistent appearance across various designs by utilizing saved layer patterns. This is particularly advantageous when employing templates or branding. Apply the desirable effects to a layer and save it as a preset to save a style. Subsequently, this style can be implemented on additional layers to guarantee uniformity in design. This method guarantees that each project maintains the same visual quality, thereby increasing the efficiency and cohesiveness of the design process. Additionally, it saves time.

Tips for Layer Usage

Mastering the utilization of layers is essential for optimizing design efficacy in CorelDRAW. Users can optimize their productivity and expedite their workflow by organizing intricate projects and employing shortcut keys.

Layer Tips for Complex Projects

The effective organization of layers is essential when working on intricate projects in CorelDRAW. Users should establish distinct layers for various elements, such as text, background, and images. This method allows for the editing of each component without influencing the others. Layers are also easier to manage when they are named descriptively. Users have the option to alter the default designations, such as Layer 1 or Layer 2, to a more specific name. For example, the identification of layers is significantly expedited by the use of names such as "Background," "Text," or "Icons." An additional recommendation is to capitalize on categorizing. Users can simultaneously manipulate multiple elements by grouping related objects on a single layer. This is notably beneficial for the simultaneous movement or scaling of multiple objects. Master layers can also be advantageous, as they facilitate the uniformity of elements across numerous pages.

Shortcut Keys for Layers Management

The layer management process can be substantially expedited by employing shortcuts in CorelDRAW. Common shortcuts include the following: tapping **Ctrl + D** to duplicate an object or layer and **Ctrl + A** to select all objects on a layer. The **Eye icon** in the Objects docker can be utilized by users to rapidly hide or display layers. **Page Up** and **Page Down** are convenient for moving objects up or down the layer hierarchy when transitioning between layers. Furthermore, the **Shift + Click** shortcut can select multiple layers simultaneously, thereby improving the efficacy of multitasking. By comprehending these shortcuts, users can operate more efficiently, thereby facilitating the layers management process in CorelDRAW more intuitively and seamlessly.

Troubleshooting Layer Issues

Working with layers in CorelDRAW can occasionally be a challenge. Understanding how to resolve common issues and recover deleted layers is essential for ensuring a seamless workflow.

Solving Common Layer Problems

Occasionally, users encounter problems such as objects not functioning as anticipated or layers not appearing. Begin by verifying that the **Object Manager** or **Objects docker** is opened. Layer management can be challenging without it. Navigate to **Window > Dockers > Object Manager** on Windows or **Window > Inspectors > Objects on Mac.** Layer visibility should be verified if they are still absent. Ensure that the eye icon adjacent to each layer is visible, as it determines whether the contents of the layer are displayed. Verify that the layer is unlocked if objects appear to be immobilized. Layers that are locked are incapable of undergoing modifications or selections. At times, strata can be placed above or below other objects without justification. Utilize drag and drop to rearrange layers, which can resolve visibility concerns. Users who are experiencing unanticipated layer behavior may find it advantageous to establish new layers to isolate the issue.

Recovering Lost Layers

The act of inadvertently deleting layers can be concerning; however, there is potential for recovery. Press **Ctrl + Z** on Windows or **Command + Z** on Mac to promptly utilize the **Undo** function. As long as no other actions have overwritten them, this action can rapidly restore expunged items. It is essential to consistently save progress for individuals who encounter frequent issues. Utilize the **Save As** function to preserve various variants of your work. These files can function as backups if layers are irrevocably lost. Experimenting with the Object Manager docker to identify any concealed layers within the document is also beneficial. Initially, hidden layers can appear to be absent; however, they can be reactivated by adjusting their visibility.

CHAPTER NINE
PRINT AND EXPORT

Preparing Your Design for Print

Set Up Your Document Correctly

Configuring the document settings correctly at the outset of your project is the initial step in preparing your design for print. Begin by selecting the appropriate **page size** and **orientation** for your intended output, whether it be a poster, flier, or business card. Navigate to **File > New Document** and select the precise dimensions of your project. A4, A5, or custom dimensions are the most frequently used measurements, contingent upon the specific printing needs. Ensure that you adhere to the printer's preferred units of measurement (e.g., millimeters or inches) to ensure accurate alignment. Ensure that your document has sufficient **bleed margins**, which are typically 3–5 mm beyond the document's edge. Bleed is a critical component of designs that extend to the margin of the printed material, as it prevents the occurrence of unintentional white borders that can result from minor trimming inaccuracies. You have the option to establish bleed margins in the document settings or manually extend your design elements beyond the page boundary.

Choose the Right Color Mode

The **CMYK color model** (Cyan, Magenta, Yellow, and Black) is employed in printed materials, as opposed to the RGB model that is employed on digital displays. Before commencing your design, verify that your document is configured in CMYK mode. Navigate to **Tools > Color Management > Default Settings** and select **CMYK** as the principal color mode. Ensure that the images are in CMYK mode when working with them. The colors of images in RGB may appear vibrant on the screen, but they may appear drab or attenuated when converted to CMYK for printing. To convert images to CMYK, select them and navigate to **Bitmaps > Convert to Bitmap**, ensuring that the color mode is set to **CMYK**.

Ensure High-Resolution Graphics

To preserve clarity and precision, print initiatives necessitate high-resolution images and elements. **300 DPI (dots per inch)** or higher is the industry standard for print resolution. The final output may exhibit pixelation or blurriness due to images with reduced resolutions. To verify the DPI of an image in CorelDRAW, select the image and navigate to **Bitmaps > Resample**. Resize the image, if necessary, but refrain from scaling up low-resolution images excessively, as this can result in a decrease in quality. When it comes to vector graphics, resolution is not an issue, as they are resolution-independent and can be scaled without sacrificing quality. Guarantee that all vector elements, including logos and images, are either generated or imported in vector format.

Embed Fonts and Outline Text

Special attention must be given to the text in your design to guarantee that it prints accurately. Certain printers cannot have access to the fonts utilized in your design, which can result in substitution errors and potentially alter the final appearance. **To avert this, you have two alternatives:**

1. **Embed Fonts:** Ensure that typefaces are embedded in formats such as PDF when exporting your file. This guarantees the precise depiction of the font data during the printing process.
2. **Convert Text to Curves:** To enhance the security of your design, it is recommended that you convert all text to curves before finalizing it. Select the text and then navigate to **Object > Convert to Curves (Ctrl+Q)**. This eliminates font dependency by converting the text into vector shapes. It is important to note that text that has been converted to curves is no longer modifiable. Therefore, it is imperative to complete all necessary proofreading before implementing this procedure.

Add Crop Marks and Bleeds

Professional printing necessitates crop markings and bleeding. The bleed area guarantees that no unintended white margins will appear after trimming, while Crop marks indicate the specific location where the paper will be trimmed. To include crop marks and bleeds in CorelDRAW, navigate to **File > Publish to PDF** and activate the crop marks and bleeding options in the export settings. Ensure that your design elements extend beyond the bleed area to account for any discrepancies in the trimming process.

Check Colors and Spot Colors

Spot colors should be employed instead of CMYK blends for designs that necessitate precise color reproduction, such as logos or branding materials. Spot colors, such as those from the Pantone Matching System (PMS), offer pre-mixed pigments that are consistent and precise for color matching. The **Color Palette Manager** in CorelDRAW allows you to apply spot colors by selecting an object and selecting a Pantone color. To prevent inconsistencies, it is important to flatten or rasterize gradients, transparency, or shadows in your design before printing, as certain printing systems may not be able to accurately manage these effects.

Proof your Design

Thoroughly verify your design for errors before its completion. Check for inconsistencies, alignment issues, missing elements, and proper spacing. Utilize CorelDRAW's **Preflight Tool** to detect potential issues, including color inconsistencies or low-resolution images. Review the report for any issues that require resolution by accessing the utility through **File > Preflight**.

Exporting Your File

It is imperative to export your design in the appropriate format to ensure compatibility and quality. PDF/X standards, such as PDF/X-1a or PDF/X-4, are the most frequently used printing format. These standards guarantee that all fonts, images, and colors are preserved and optimized for print. To export your file, navigate to **File > Publish to PDF** and select the appropriate PDF/X standard. Enable the ability to embed fonts, preserve vector data, and include bleed and crop marks. Additionally, it is possible to export files in alternative formats, such as TIFF or EPS, for collaboration or specialty printing. Before exporting, verify that all essential settings, including color mode and resolution, are properly configured.

Test Printing

Before conducting a complete print run, it is advisable to obtain a test print or proof from your printer, if feasible. Verifying the accuracy of colors, layout, and resolution is possible through test printing. If any discrepancies arise, you can make the necessary adjustments and re-export the file.

Exporting for Web and Digital Media

Ensure that your design is optimized for digital use before exporting. CorelDRAW provides tools to assist you in customizing your project to meet the needs of digital and web platforms. Begin by verifying the specifications of your document. Typically, the RGB color format is employed in digital designs because it is consistent with how colors are displayed on displays. To convert your project to RGB, navigate to **Tools > Color Management > Default Settings** and select **RGB** as the principal color model if it is presently in CMYK mode (common for print). Another critical factor for digital media is resolution. Screens do not necessitate the high resolution necessary for print, so a resolution of **72 DPI (dots per inch)** is adequate for the majority of web graphics. Nevertheless, a resolution of 150 DPI or higher can be necessary if your design is intended for high-density displays, such as Retina screens. In CorelDRAW, you can modify the resolution settings by selecting **Bitmaps > Resample**. This will allow you to specify the desired DPI.

Choosing the Right File Format

The selection of file format is contingent upon the nature of the digital media and its intended use. **CorelDRAW offers a diverse selection of formats for exporting designs to the web and other digital platforms, each with its unique advantages:**
- **JPEG:** JPEG is the optimal format for complex images with gradients and photographs. It strikes an appropriate equilibrium between file size and quality. Utilize this format for background images, social media posts, and banners.
- **PNG:** This is the most suitable format for graphics that necessitate precise margins, such as logos, icons, and illustrations, and supports transparency. When transparency is imperative, PNG is the preferred format.
- **SVG:** A vector-based format that maintains its fidelity when resized. This format is suitable for logos, icons, and illustrations on websites, as it guarantees their clarity on all screen resolutions.
- **GIF:** Utilized for small graphics or basic animations with restricted color palettes. It is appropriate for web animations that are low-resolution.
- **PDF:** Although PDFs are predominantly regarded as a print format, they can be optimized for digital use, particularly for online document sharing.
- **WebP:** A contemporary format that is optimized for websites and applications that necessitate rapid launching, while simultaneously preserving high quality.

To export your design, navigate to **File > Export** and select the desired format. CorelDRAW offers customization options, including the ability to alter compression levels, transparency, and resolution, depending on the selected format.

Optimizing File Size

Web and digital media necessitate careful consideration of file size. The user experience and SEO rankings **can be adversely affected by the sluggish rendering times of websites caused by large files. CorelDRAW provides tools to optimize file size during export:**

1. **Compression:** To achieve a balance between file size and quality, modify the compression quality slider for JPEGs. The file size is reduced by using lower compression values; however, this can result in the introduction of visible anomalies.
2. **Transparency:** To prevent unnecessary file growth, ensure that transparency is only implemented where necessary when using PNGs.
3. **Resizing:** Export images at the precise dimensions required for their intended purpose. The file size is unduly increased by oversized images. Before exporting, utilize **Bitmaps > Resample** to resize your design.
4. **Remove Unused Elements:** Before exporting, eliminate any concealed layers or off-canvas elements to simplify the file.

Exporting for Social Media

When creating designs for social media platforms, it is important to take into account the unique file requirements and dimensions of each platform. CorelDRAW enables you to generate designs that are customized to these requirements and export them in the corresponding format.
For example,

- The standard format for Instagram posts is a square of **1080 x 1080 px**.
- Facebook cover photos necessitate dimensions of **851 x 315 px**.
- **1584 x 396 px** is a common size for LinkedIn banners.

Set the page size to the desired dimensions in **Layout > Page Setup** to personalize your design for a particular platform. Upon completion of the design, export it as a PNG or JPEG, contingent upon the platform's preferences.

Using Export Options

Advanced options are available in CorelDRAW's export dialog to improve the quality of your output for digital media. **Pay close attention to the subsequent configurations when exporting:**

1. **Resolution:** For standard web graphics, set the **DPI** to **72**, or higher for high-resolution displays.
2. **Anti-Aliasing:** Enable anti-aliasing to enhance the appearance of text and shapes by smoothing edges.
3. **Background Transparency:** To enable transparency in the export settings for graphics that necessitate a transparent background, such as logos, select **PNG** or **SVG**.
4. **Metadata:** To optimize the exported file for online use using search engine optimization (SEO), it is necessary to include metadata (e.g., title, description, and keywords).

Exporting SVG for Scalable Graphics

SVG is the optimal format for scalable visuals, such as logos and icons. It is lightweight for web use and maintains resolution across all screen sizes. You can export an SVG in CorelDRAW by selecting **File > Export > SVG**. **Select the subsequent settings in the export dialog:**

- Enable **Preserve Editable Objects** to maintain the integrity of vector data.
- If your design incorporates personalized typography, select **Embed Fonts**.

- Reduce the file size by disabling superfluous attributes, such as concealed layers or unused effects.

Previewing and Testing Your Exported Design

To guarantee that your design appears as intended, evaluate it on various devices and screen sizes after exporting it. Check for issues such as resolution, alignment, or color fidelity by opening your exported file on a desktop monitor, a smartphone, or a tablet. Additionally, it is imperative to evaluate your design on its intended platform. For instance, to verify that a banner is displayed accurately, upload it to a website or post it to a social media platform. Return to CorelDRAW, make the necessary modifications, and re-export the file if necessary.

Troubleshooting Print and Export Issues

Resolving Print Issues

Color Mismatches

One of the most prevalent issues is that colors appear differently in print than they do on screen. This is frequently the result of discrepancies between the **CMYK (print)** and **RGB (screen)** color models. RGB colors are vivid on digital displays; however, they may not be precisely reproduced in CMYK. When designing for print, it is imperative to operate in **CMYK color mode**. To convert your document to CMYK, navigate to **Tools > Color Management > Default Settings** and verify that all images and objects are set to CMYK. If you are collaborating with a particular printer, request their ICC (International Color Consortium) profile and incorporate it into your design to simulate the appearance of the colors when printed. To evaluate the print output on your screen, utilize **soft proofing (View > Proof Colors)**.

Blurry or Pixelated Print Output

The utilization of low-resolution graphics results in images that are pixelated or blurry. Images must have a resolution of at least **300 DPI (dots per inch)** to produce high-quality reproductions. In CorelDRAW, you can verify and modify the resolution of an image by selecting it and proceeding to **Bitmaps > Resample**. If the resolution of your images is less than 300 DPI, you may want to consider substituting them with higher-resolution versions or scaling them down in your design.

Missing or Substituted Fonts

If the typefaces appear differently in print, probably, the printer does not have the fonts you utilized. To prevent this, either embed fonts during export or convert text to curves. The process of converting text to curves guarantees that the text remains unaltered as it is transformed into vector shapes. To convert text to curves, select the text and then navigate to **Object > Convert to Curves (Ctrl+Q)**. Please be advised that the text that has been converted is no longer modifiable. Therefore, it is imperative to verify any errors before implementing this procedure.

Incomplete or Cropped Prints

The absence or cropping of certain components of your design in the final print can be the result of inadequate bleed or inaccurate margins. To account for pruning errors, it is imperative to include **bleed margins** that extend 3–5 mm beyond the boundaries of your design. To include bleed during export, ensure that it is enabled in the PDF export settings under **File > Publish to PDF > Settings**.

Transparency and Shadow Issues

Transparency, gradients, and shadows are difficult to render accurately on certain printers. To resolve this issue, it is necessary to normalize transparency effects before exporting. Select the object with transparency, then navigate to **Bitmaps > Convert to Bitmap**, and select **300 DPI** with a CMYK color mode. This will ensure that the effects are printed as intended by rasterizing them.

Resolving Export Issues

File Format Incompatibility

An unsupported format or incorrect settings can be the cause of your exported file not being able to be accessed or used as intended. It is imperative to verify the necessary file format with your client or intended platform. To guarantee compatibility with professional printers, export as **PDF/X-1a** or **PDF/X-4** for printing purposes. Formats such as **JPEG, PNG, SVG, or WebP** are more appropriate for digital media. To ensure a successful export, navigate to **File > Export**, select the desired format, and adjust the settings to align with the intended purpose. If the exported file continues to malfunction, consider re-exporting it with alternative settings, such as embedding fonts or flattening transparency.

Large File Sizes

Excessively massive exported files can impede workflows or render transfers impractical. To decrease the size of the file:
- **Compress Images:** Utilize the export settings to optimize image compression. To reduce the size of JPEGs without the presence of a perceptible quality loss, marginally reduce the quality.
- **Limit Resolution:** For digital or web applications, establish a resolution of 72 DPI. Utilize a **DPI** of **150** for displays with a high resolution.
- **Flatten Layers:** Reduce the number of superfluous layers and effects in your file by flattening them. To optimize the file, merge objects and convert transparency effects to bitmaps.

Poor Image Quality in Exported Files

Incorrect resolution or scaling during export can be the cause of images appearing indistinct or distorted in your exported file. It is imperative to export at the same dimensions as the intended output. Before exporting, resize your design in CorelDRAW to align with the intended export dimensions. For print purposes, ensure that the export dialog's resolution is set to a minimum of **300 DPI**, and for digital use, select the appropriate DPI.

Missing Elements in Exported Files

Certain objects or layers can be concealed or sealed during the export process, resulting in the absence of certain elements. Ensure that all essential layers are visible and accessible in the **Object Manager** before exporting. Furthermore, ensure that no objects are positioned beyond the page boundaries of the document unless they are specifically intentionally excluded.

Transparency Issues in Exported Files

When exporting files with effects such as shadows, gradients, or transparent objects, transparency issues, such as banding or unanticipated colors, frequently occur. To resolve this issue, convert transparency effects to bitmaps to flatten them. Go to Bitmaps > Convert to Bitmap, select the object with transparency, and select the settings that correspond to your output requirements (e.g., 300 DPI for print or 72 DPI for web).

General Troubleshooting Tips

1. **Use Preflight Tools:** CorelDRAW includes a **Preflight Tool** that detects potential issues before printing or exporting. Review the generated report for any issues, such as missing fonts, incorrect color modes, or low-resolution images, by navigating to **File > Preflight.**
2. **Test Small Sections:** To evaluate the rendering of intricate designs, export or print a small section. This can assist in the early identification of issues, enabling you to make corrections before the finalization of the entire design.
3. **Update Software:** Guarantee that your printer drivers and CorelDRAW 2025 are current. Compatibility issues or defects may arise during the printing and exporting processes as a result of outdated software.
4. **Collaborate with Printers:** When collaborating with a professional printer, it is important to communicate your design specifications and inquire about their preferred file settings. To guarantee optimal outcomes, they can furnish templates or particular instructions.
5. **Preview Output:** Utilize CorelDRAW's **Proof Colors** feature to visualize the appearance of colors in print. In the same vein, guarantee that exported files are displayed accurately by previewing them in their intended environment, such as a web browser or PDF viewer.

CHAPTER TEN

KEYBOARD SHORTCUTS

Basic File Operations

- **Ctrl + N**: Create a new document
- **Ctrl + O**: Open an existing document
- **Ctrl + S**: Save the current document

- **Ctrl + Shift + S**: Save As
- **Ctrl + P**: Print
- **Ctrl + Q**: Quit CorelDRAW
- **Ctrl + Z**: Undo
- **Ctrl + Y**: Redo

Selection and Navigation

- **Ctrl + A**: Select all objects
- **Tab**: Select the next object
- **Shift + Tab**: Select the previous object
- **Ctrl + Click**: Select multiple objects
- **Alt + Click**: Select an object behind another

View and Zoom Controls

- **Ctrl + 1**: Zoom to 100%
- **F4**: Zoom to all objects
- **Shift + F2**: Zoom to selected objects
- **Ctrl + F2**: Zoom to page width
- **Alt + Z**: Toggle Zoom Tool

Drawing and Editing Tools

- **F5**: Activate Freehand Tool
- **F6**: Activate Rectangle Tool
- **F7**: Activate Ellipse Tool
- **F8**: Activate Text Tool
- **Ctrl + Q**: Convert to Curves
- **Ctrl + K**: Break apart objects
- **Ctrl + L**: Combine objects
- **Ctrl + Shift + Q**: Convert outline to object

Color and Fill

- **Shift + F11**: Open Fill dialog box
- **Shift + F12**: Open Outline Pen dialog box
- **Ctrl + F11**: Open Fountain Fill dialog box
- **Ctrl + Shift + F11**: Open Texture Fill dialog box

Alignment and Arrangement

- **Ctrl + Shift + T**: Align to top
- **Ctrl + Shift + B**: Align to bottom
- **Ctrl + Shift + L**: Align to the left
- **Ctrl + Shift + R**: Align to right
- **Ctrl + Shift + C**: Align to center
- **Ctrl + Shift + E**: Align to horizontally center

PowerClip and Effects

- **Ctrl + Shift + P**: Place object inside PowerClip frame
- **Ctrl + Alt + P**: Edit PowerClip
- **Ctrl + F9**: Open the Effects Docker

Text Editing

- **Ctrl + T**: Open the Text Properties Docker
- **Ctrl + Shift + P**: Change font size
- **Ctrl + B**: Bold text
- **Ctrl + I**: Italicize text
- **Ctrl + U**: Underline text
- **Ctrl + K**: Break apart text

Page and Layout Controls

- **Ctrl + Shift + N**: Add a new page
- **Ctrl + Page Up**: Go to the previous page
- **Ctrl + Page Down**: Go to the next page
- **Ctrl + Shift + L**: Open the Layout Docker

Bitmaps

- **Ctrl + B**: Convert to Bitmap
- **Alt + B**: Open Bitmap Options
- **Ctrl + Shift + B**: Resample Bitmap

Customization and Preferences

- **Ctrl + J**: Open the Options dialog box
- **Ctrl + R**: Repeat the last action

- **Alt + F7**: Open Object Styles Docker

Object Manipulation

- **Ctrl + D**: Duplicate selected object
- **Ctrl + Shift + D**: Duplicate and place inline
- **Ctrl + G**: Group selected objects
- **Ctrl + U**: Ungroup selected objects
- **Ctrl + Shift + Z**: Bring the object to front
- **Ctrl + Shift + X**: Send object to back

Guides and Rulers

- **Ctrl + R**: Show or hide rulers
- **Alt + F7**: Open Guidelines Docker
- **Shift + R**: Add a horizontal guideline
- **Shift + Alt + R**: Add a vertical guideline

Export and Import

- **Ctrl + E**: Export
- **Ctrl + I**: Import
- **Ctrl + Shift + E**: Export for web

CHAPTER ELEVEN

TROUBLESHOOTING AND FAQS

How to Resolve Common Issues

Performance Issues

Performance problems, such as slow response times, freezing, or crashes, often stem from the complexity of the design file, insufficient system resources, or outdated software. Large projects with many objects, layers, and effects can strain CorelDRAW, especially on lower-end systems. Begin by optimizing your design to resolve performance issues. Decrease the quantity of superfluous objects, layers, and nodes. For instance, if your design includes numerous small shapes or complex paths, you can simplify them by employing the **Reduce Nodes** option in the **Shape Tool.** The **Weld Tool** can also be used to reduce the complexity of files by consolidating numerous overlapping objects. Another method is to utilize reduced file sizes. Refrain from directly incorporating high-resolution, large images into your project. Rather, utilize the **Linked Images** feature to link to images whenever feasible, which will reduce the file size of your CorelDRAW document. Verify that the images are resampled to the appropriate DPI (300 DPI for print or 72 DPI for web) using **Bitmaps > Resample** if high-resolution images are necessary. Furthermore, verify the performance settings of your system. Ensure that your computer satisfies or exceeds the recommended hardware requirements for CorelDRAW, which include a dedicated graphics card and sufficient RAM. To liberate system resources, close unnecessary background applications. By consistently updating CorelDRAW to the most recent version, you can take advantage of the optimization enhancements and problem fixes that have been released by the developers.

Font-Related Problems

Font issues are frequently encountered in CorelDRAW, particularly when files are opened on a system that lacks the original fonts. The appearance of a design can be significantly impacted by the absence or substitution of fonts. CorelDRAW offers a **Font Substitution Dialog** that is revealed when a font is absent to resolve this issue. Replace the missing font with an installed font or install the missing typeface if you have access to it using this dialog. Alternatively, you can convert all text to curves before sharing your file with others. To accomplish this, select the text and then navigate to **Object > Convert to Curves (Ctrl+Q)**. This guarantees that the text maintains its appearance, but it renders it uneditable. Consider using **Corel Font Manager** to organize your typefaces if you encounter performance issues or problems when working with a large number of fonts. This utility facilitates the management of active and inactive typefaces, thereby alleviating the burden on CorelDRAW during font loading. Streamline operations by activating only the fonts that are required for your project.

Color Mismatches

Color discrepancies between the design on the screen and the printed output are a common issue. This problem is the result of discrepancies in device calibration and color models (RGB for displays and CMYK for print). Always operate in the appropriate color mode for your endeavor to rectify color discrepancies. To ensure that your document is in CMYK mode for print designs, navigate to **Tools > Color Management > Default Settings** and select **CMYK**. Make use of the **Proof Colors** option in the View menu to simulate the appearance of colors in print. Request the specific profile from your print provider and apply it to your document if your printer supports ICC profiles. This guarantees that the printer's particular configuration interprets colors accurately. Spot colors, such as those from the Pantone Matching System, are recommended for designs that necessitate precise color matching, such as branding.

Crashing or File Corruption

Lost progress and frustration can be the consequence of file corruption or frequent failures. Corrupted files are frequently the result of software errors, unexpected shutdowns, or the storing of files on unstable storage devices. To prevent corruption, it is recommended that you save your work frequently and generate multiple versions of your file using the **Save As** feature. Periodic backups are guaranteed by activating CorelDRAW's Auto-Save feature under **Tools > Options > Workspace > Save**. CorelDRAW initiates Recovery Mode when it detects a problem, which can be used to access a corrupted file. Alternatively, the contents of the corrupted file can be recovered by importing it into a new document. If CorelDRAW malfunctions frequently ensure that your software is current. Instability may result from unresolved flaws in outdated versions. Your graphics and operating system drivers must be up-to-date, as antiquated drivers can cause compatibility issues with CorelDRAW.

Transparency and Effect Issues

When exporting designs or preparing files for print, it is common to encounter issues with transparency, gradients, or other effects. For instance, transparent objects can appear distorted in exported files or appear differently in print. To resolve this issue, it is necessary to convert transparency effects to bitmaps before exporting. Select the objects that are affected, navigate to **Bitmaps > Convert to Bitmap**, and select the appropriate color mode and resolution. The final output is guaranteed to reflect the intended effects as a result of this process. Verify that the file format you have selected supports transparency to resolve any export issues. Formats such as PNG and PDF/X-4 are optimal for maintaining transparency.

Tool Malfunctions or Unexpected Behavior

This may be the result of a temporary software malfunction or misconfigured settings in CorelDRAW if the tools are not functioning as anticipated. Objects cannot be selected accurately by the Pick Tool, and the Shape Tool cannot be able to modify trajectories. To initiate troubleshooting, CorelDRAW should be reset to its default settings. Press and hold the **F8** on your keyboard while the software is launched, and approve the reset when prompted. This reverts all tools and preferences to their original factory settings. If the problem persists, verify that the tool is configured correctly by reviewing the **Docker Settings** and **Property Bar**. For instance, if the Freehand Tool generates irregular lines, modify the **Smoothing** setting in the Property Bar. In the same vein, verify that snapping options such as Snap to Guidelines or Snap to Objects are appropriately enabled or disabled, contingent upon your requirements.

Export Problems

Workflows can be disrupted by exporting issues, including incompatible file formats, poor resolution, or missing elements. Verify that all layers are visible and accessible in the **Object Manager Docker** to guarantee that all elements are included in the exported file. Unless explicitly included, objects that are located outside the page boundaries will not be included in exports. When designs are exported at a low DPI, resolution issues arise. When exporting files, ensure that the resolution is set to **300 DPI** for print or **72 DPI** for web. To prevent scaling issues, ensure that the output dimensions of rasterized designs, such as JPEGs or PNGs, correspond to the intended use. To resolve compatibility concerns, choose the appropriate file format for your project. Utilize **PDF/X** standards for printing purposes to guarantee compatibility with professional printers. Formats such as **PNG, SVG, or WebP** are more suitable for digital or web designs.

Optimizing Performance in CorelDRAW

Managing Files and Reducing Complexity

Especially when they contain numerous objects, layers, or high-resolution images, CorelDRAW can be taxed by large and intricate files. Manage the complexity of your designs and reduce the number of superfluous elements in your files to simplify them. Begin by organizing objects that are related. CorelDRAW can enhance rendering performance by reducing the number of individual elements it processes through grouping. For example, rather than maintaining hundreds of small shapes as individual objects, employ the **Group Tool (Ctrl + G)** to combine them into a single group. Reduce the number of nodes in vector graphics with complex paths by employing the **Shape Tool**. To simplify the shape without sacrificing its appearance, select a path and click **Reduce Nodes** in the Property Bar. This is particularly beneficial for objects that were generated using tracing tools or imported SVGs. The efficacy of your project can be impeded by the inclusion of large bitmap images. Rather than embedding images, link them by selecting **Import**, selecting the image, and enabling the **Link Image** option in the import dialog. This ensures that the image is accessible for modification while simultaneously reducing the file size. Convert final text objects to curves **(Ctrl + Q)** when working with text if they no longer necessitate editing. This mitigates the processing burden associated with modifiable text formatting.

Optimizing Display and Rendering Settings

CorelDRAW features the ability to modify display and rendering settings to achieve a harmonious equilibrium between visual quality and performance. For instance, the **Enhanced View** mode renders objects with high-quality anti-aliasing, but it can put a strain on your system when dealing with large files. Switch to Wireframe View to expedite the revision and navigation of intricate designs. The **View** menu provides the ability to modify the view mode. Depending on the characteristics of your system, either enable or disable **GPU acceleration**. GPU acceleration can enhance the efficacy of scanning and rendering; however, it may result in instability in certain systems. To activate this feature, navigate to **Tools > Options > Global > Display** and modify the hardware acceleration settings. The processing burden can also be reduced by adjusting the **Object Hinting** and **Dynamic Guides** settings. Although these features are beneficial for precision alignment, temporarily disabling them when working with numerous objects can enhance performance. Navigate to **Tools > Options > Workspace > Snap to Objects** to access these settings.

Workspace Customization for Efficiency

The efficacy of software and your productivity can be impeded by a congested workspace. Modify your workspace by eliminating panels, dockers, or tools that are not in use. To disable toolbars that are not routinely used, navigate to **Window > Toolbars**. CorelDRAW can allocate resources to active tools and processes by streamlining your workspace, which reduces distractions. Preserve frequently used settings as part of a personalized workspace. This ensures consistency in your productivity and eliminates the necessity of repeatedly configuring preferences. Export your settings by navigating to **Tools > Options > Workspace** to save a custom workspace.

File Saving and Auto-Backup

Your workflow can be disrupted by frequent auto-saving, particularly when dealing with larger files. Under **Tools > Options > Workspace > Save**, modify the auto-save interval to an extended duration. Nevertheless, it is crucial to maintain auto-save to prevent data loss. Consider storing incremental versions manually using **Save As** with version numbers (e.g., **Project_v1, Project_v2**) for exceedingly large files. In the save dialog, select the **Compress File** option to enable file compression for CorelDRAW files. This optimizes the efficiency of saving operations and minimizes the size of the file.

Managing Color Profiles and Effects

Performance can also be influenced by color management settings, particularly in projects that incorporate multiple color profiles or effects such as gradients and transparency. Simplify color administration by employing a single color profile for the entire document. Navigate to **Tools > Color Management > Document Settings** and select the appropriate profile (e.g., RGB for web or CMYK for print). Rendering performance can be substantially enhanced by flattening transparency effects. Select the desired resolution and color mode when converting objects with complex transparency or gradients to bitmaps using **Bitmaps > Convert to Bitmap**. Avoid the overuse of live effects, such as artistic filters or drop shadows. As you modify your design, these effects necessitate continuous recalculation. Rasterize or incorporate the effect into the design once it has been finalized to free up processing power.

Testing and Repairing CorelDRAW

Perform a performance test on your CorelDRAW installation if such issues persist. While launching CorelDRAW, operate the software in Safe Mode by pressing F8. This can rectify issues caused by corrupted preferences or customizations by resetting the software to its default settings. Consistently verify and implement updates by accessing **Help > Updates**. CorelDRAW frequently publishes patches and updates to enhance performance and resolve problems. If CorelDRAW malfunctions or displays peculiar behavior, utilize the **Repair** option that is accessible in the installation wizard. To access it, execute the installer and select the **Repair Installation** option. This resolves corrupted files without affecting your stored projects.

Best Practices for Optimized Performance

To maintain optimal performance in CorelDRAW:
- Periodically restart the software to purge the cache during extended sessions.
- Prevent the simultaneous access of multiple sizable files unless it is necessary.
- Regularly delete transient files on your system to free up disk space.
- To alleviate the burden on your primary drive, utilize external storage devices for archival files and backups.

Understanding Error Messages

When CorelDRAW encounters situations that it is unable to process due to internal errors, incompatible file formats, absent resources, or user errors, error messages are typically displayed. These messages are the software's method of notifying you of an issue and frequently include descriptions that assist in comprehending the problem. While some errors are trivial and can be readily resolved, others may necessitate more sophisticated troubleshooting.

Common Error Messages and Their Resolutions

1. **File Corrupt or Cannot Be Opened**

This error occurs when CorelDRAW is unable to open a file due to its incompatible format or damage.
- **Cause:** Unanticipated interruptions during the saving process, such as power disruptions, file format incompatibility, or storing to unstable storage devices.
- **Solution:**
- o Attempt to access the file by selecting the Import option instead of Access. Navigate to **File > Import**, select the file, and verify that it can be imported into a new document.
- o If feasible, utilize a backup copy of the file or consult the auto-save folder for the most recent iterations.
- o Recovery software that is specifically developed to repair CorelDRAW files should be employed for minor corruption. If the attempt is unsuccessful, please contact Corel's support team for additional assistance.

2. **Out of Memory**

This error suggests that the operation or file you are currently working on is not being adequately supported by your system's resources.
- **Cause:** Excessive use of effects such as transparency and gradients, limited system RAM, or large or complex files.
- **Solution:**
  - o Close applications that are not necessary to free up system memory.
  - o Divide your design into smaller components by dividing it into multiple files.
  - o Simplify vector shapes (e.g., by utilizing the **Reduce Nodes** feature in the Shape Tool) or convert effects to bitmaps **(Bitmaps > Convert to Bitmap)** to reduce file complexity.
  - o If memory errors persist, consider upgrading your system with a more potent processor or additional RAM.

3. **Font Not Found**

This message is displayed when a file contains fonts that are not installed on your system.
- **Cause:** Missing fonts that were used in the design.

- **Solution:**
  - o Use the **Font Substitution Dialog** to replace the missing font with an alternative or install the missing typeface if you have access to it when prompted.
  - o To prevent font dependency, convert text to curves **(Ctrl + Q)** before sharing files with others. It is important to note that text that has been converted to curves is no longer editable.

4. **Unsupported File Format**

This error occurs when CorelDRAW is unable to distinguish the file type being attempted to be opened or imported.

- **Cause:** The attempt to open a file that was generated in another program without the appropriate conversion or using an unsupported format.
- **Solution:**
  - o Verify that the file is in a format that is compatible with CorelDRAW, such as CDR, AI, EPS, SVG, or PDF. If not, utilize third-party software to convert it to a compatible format.
  - o To guarantee compatibility with older versions of CorelDRAW, select an older CDR format by utilizing **File > Save As** in the latest version of CorelDRAW.

5. **An Unrecoverable Error Has Occurred**

This error message is generally indicative of a breakdown or a severe issue that CorelDRAW was unable to resolve.

- **Cause:** Corrupted preferences, system instability, or software bugs.
- **Solution:**
  - o Restart CorelDRAW and attempt to reproduce the issue to determine the precise cause.
  - o To launch CorelDRAW in **Safe Mode**, press and hold **F8** during the startup process. This will restore the settings to their default state and disable any extensions.
  - o Ensure that you are using the most recent version of CorelDRAW, as updates frequently resolve known bugs.

6. **Transparency or Effects Not Supported**

This error occurs when a file that contains sophisticated effects, such as gradients or transparency, is exported or printed.

- **Cause:** Complex effects cannot be supported by specific file formats or print drivers.
- **Solution:**
  - o Convert objects to bitmaps to flatten transparency or rasterize effects. Navigate to **Bitmaps > Convert to Bitmap** and select the appropriate color mode and resolution.
  - o When exporting, select a file format that supports transparency, such as PNG or PDF/X-4.

7. **Object Outside the Printable Area**

- **Cause:** Objects are positioned outside the page margins or overflow area.
- **Solution:**
  - o Verify that all necessary components are contained within the printable area by examining the **Print Preview.**
  - o If the design is intended to extend beyond the page, either move objects within the document's boundaries or enable the bleed option in your document settings.

8. **Invalid Input**

During an operation, this error is triggered when an unsupported or incorrect command is entered.

- **Cause:** Unsupported actions, incorrect settings, or typographical errors.
- **Solution:**
  - o Consult CorelDRAW's documentation for the correct procedure and verify the command or action you are undertaking.

○ To reset the tool settings, select the tool and then click **Reset Tool** in the Property Bar.

General Tips for Handling Error Messages

1. **Read the Error Message Carefully**: CorelDRAW's error messages frequently contain indications regarding the root cause of the problem. Pay close attention to any file names, tools, or settings that are specified.
2. **Use Safe Mode:** By holding down the **F8** key during initialization, CorelDRAW can be launched in Safe Mode, which disables customizations and reset preferences. This can assist in determining whether the issue is associated with corrupted settings or extensions.
3. **Verify for Updates:** Numerous errors are precipitated by flaws that have already been resolved in software updates. Check for updates regularly by navigating to **Help > Updates.**
4. **Test on a New Document:** If a particular file is generating errors, attempt to replicate the issue in a new document. The file may be corrupted or excessively complex if the issue does not arise.
5. **Consult CorelDRAW's Forums and Support:** CorelDRAW's community forums and official support team are invaluable resources for troubleshooting. Consult them. Numerous users provide solutions to prevalent issues that may arise.
6. **Backup Frequently:** To prevent the loss of work due to errors, it is recommended that you enable **Auto-Save** and create manual backups of your files.

FAQs

What is the difference between CorelDRAW and Corel Photo-Paint?

CorelDRAW is an excellent choice for the development of logos, pamphlets, and illustrations, as it emphasizes vector graphic design and layout. Corel Photo-Paint is a raster graphics editor that is employed for photo modification, retouching, and bitmap creation.

What is the process for converting text to curves?

To transform the text, select it and then navigate to Object > transform to Curves or use the shortcut Ctrl + Q. This ensures that the design remains consistent without font dependencies by converting the text into vector shapes.

Is it possible to use CorelDRAW for web design?

Certainly, CorelDRAW is an appropriate tool for the development of web graphics, iconography, and layouts. Ensure compatibility with web platforms by designing in RGB mode and exporting files in web-friendly formats such as PNG, SVG, or JPEG.

What is the purpose of layers in CorelDRAW?

Layers facilitate the organization of design elements by dividing objects into distinct groups, thereby simplifying the process of editing and managing intricate projects. The Object Manager Docker enables you to regulate the visibility, locking, and sequence of objects.

Why do colors look different in print than on my screen?

The utilization of RGB (screen) and CMYK (print) color models results in color variations. For print projects, it is imperative to design in CMYK and utilize Proof Colors to simulate the design's appearance when printed.

How do I reduce file size in CorelDRAW?

Grouping objects, flattening transparency effects by converting them to bitmaps, simplifying vector paths with the Shape Tool, and reducing file size by linking images instead of embedding them.

What is the difference between CorelDRAW Standard and CorelDRAW Graphics Suite?

The CorelDRAW Graphics Suite comprises sophisticated features, supplementary applications such as Corel Photo-Paint, and tools for professional design work, while CorelDRAW Standard provides fundamental tools for basic design duties.

How can I add or install fonts in CorelDRAW?

To install fonts on your system, download the font files and double-click them to initiate the installation process. The Corel Font Manager, which is a component of CorelDRAW, enables users to organize, preview, and activate fonts without the need for persistent installation.

What is the process for exporting a design for printing?

Export your design in a high-resolution format, such as PDF/X. Guarantee that your document is configured in CMYK mode, that it contains bleeds and crop marks, and that it is printed at a minimum resolution of 300 DPI to achieve high-quality results.

What is PowerClip, and how do I use it?

PowerClip is a feature that enables the placement of objects within a container shape. To confine the object within its boundaries, select the object, navigate to **Effects > PowerClip > Place inside Frame,** and click on the container.

Is it possible for CorelDRAW to open Adobe Illustrator files?

Yes, CorelDRAW is capable of opening AI files; however, certain advanced effects or features may not be accurately translated. For improved compatibility, save Illustrator files in older formats or as PDFs.

After installation, how can CorelDRAW be activated?

Upon launching CorelDRAW, you will be required to either sign in to your Corel account or input your product key to activate the software. Complete the process by adhering to the instructions that have been provided.

What are the system requirements for CorelDRAW?

A multi-core processor, 8 GB of RAM, 4 GB of unrestricted disk space, and Windows 10 or macOS 11.0 are the minimum requirements for CorelDRAW. It is advisable to utilize a more sophisticated configuration for the management of large files and advanced features.

Can I customize shortcuts in CorelDRAW?

Certainly, you can personalize shortcuts by navigating to **Tools > Options > Customization > Commands**. Choose a command, designate a new shortcut, and save your modifications.

What is the most effective method for learning CorelDRAW?

The most effective method of acquiring knowledge about CorelDRAW is to engage in practice, online video courses, and Corel's official tutorials. Developing your abilities will also be facilitated by experimenting with various tools and examining sample files.

How do I recover a corrupted CorelDRAW file?

To recover a corrupted file, attempt to import it into a new CorelDRAW document or access it in a previous version of the software. Look for versions that have been automatically saved in the backup location. If unsuccessful, use third-party recovery tools or contact Corel support.

What are the Weld, Trim, Intersect, and Combine options in CorelDRAW?

The Weld, Trim, Intersect, and Combine tools in CorelDRAW enable the manipulation of objects and the creation of new shapes by combining existing ones. The Weld option unites objects that are either overlapping or intersecting into a single shape. The Trim option eliminates the overlap between two shapes, resulting in the shared area. The Intersect option generates a new shape that is exclusively composed of the contiguous region between two shapes. The Combine option is used to combine two or more shapes into a single object.

How do I use the Weld option in CorelDRAW?

Select the objects that you wish to join to utilize the Weld feature in CorelDRAW. Navigate to the **Arrange** menu, select **Shaping**, and then select **Weld**. Alternatively, you can employ the **Weld** icon located in the **Property Bar.** To merge the objects into a single shape, merely click on the Weld button with the objects selected.

Can I use the Trim option to remove parts of an object?

Certainly, the Trim feature in CorelDRAW can be employed to eliminate portions of an object. Begin by selecting the object that requires trimming. Subsequently, choose the objects or shapes that you intend to employ as embellishments. Open the **Arrange** menu, select **Shaping**, and then select **Trim.** This will utilize the garnishes to eliminate the overlapped regions of the selected object.

How do I combine multiple objects into a single shape in CorelDRAW?

In CorelDRAW, select the objects that you wish to combine to create a singular shape. Navigate to the **Arrange** menu, select **Shaping**, and then select **Combine**. Additionally, the Property Bar offers the **Combine** option. To merge the objects into a single object, select them and click on the **Combine** icon.

Conclusion

This guide has delved into the core components of CorelDRAW 2025, including the fundamentals of vector editing and more advanced features like automation, special effects, and color management. CorelDRAW's intuitive interface is one of its most significant assets, as it enables users to effortlessly traverse intricate design processes without experiencing a sense of overwhelm. The software also incorporates a variety of AI-powered improvements that simplify repetitive duties, enabling designers to concentrate more on creativity and less on manual work. CorelDRAW 2025 provides improved collaboration tools that facilitate seamless cooperation, in addition to its comprehensive design capabilities. Users can effortlessly share their projects with clients and colleagues because of the incorporation of cloud-based storage and real-time feedback features. This makes it an ideal solution for businesses and creative teams that operate remotely. These collaboration features not only enhance productivity but also guarantee that projects are completed to the highest standards and efficiently. Users will find that mastering CorelDRAW 2025 necessitates consistent experimentation and practice. Designers can enhance their abilities and uncover new creative opportunities by consistently employing its diverse array of tools and features. Exploring online resources, such as tutorials and community forums, and remaining informed about the most recent software updates can also aid in improving one's proficiency and remaining informed about the changing design trends.

INDEX

202